SAVORING THE PEACE OF JESUS

IN A CHAOTIC WORLD

The Gospel of
JOHN

MELISSA SPOELSTRA

Lifeway Press®
Brentwood, Tennessee

ISBN: 978-1-0877-9033-6 • Item: 005843176
Dewey decimal classification: 248.843
Subject headings: WOMEN \ BIBLE. N.T. JOHN--STUDY AND TEACHING \ CHRISTIAN LIFE

To order additional copies of this resource, write to Lifeway Resources Customer Service; 200 Powell Place, Suite 100; Brentwood, TN 37027-7707; order online at www.lifeway.com; fax 615.251.5933; phone toll free 800.458.2772; or email orderentry@lifeway.com.

Printed in the United States of America

Lifeway Women Bible Studies • Lifeway Resources
200 Powell Place, Suite 100 • Brentwood, TN 37027-7707

Cover art by Lauren Ervin

Author photo by Chrissy Nix Photography

EDITORIAL TEAM, LIFEWAY WOMEN BIBLE STUDIES

Becky Loyd
Director, Lifeway Women

Tina Boesch
Manager

Chelsea Waack
Production Leader

Mike Wakefield
Content Editor

Lindsey Bush
Production Editor

Lauren Ervin
Art Director

Sarah Hobbs
Graphic Designer

Contents

About the Author

Melissa Spoelstra is a women's conference speaker, Bible teacher, and author who is madly in love with Jesus and passionate about studying God's Word and helping women of all ages to seek Christ and know Him more intimately through serious Bible study. Melissa has a degree in Bible theology and is the author of the Bible studies *Isaiah: Striving Less and Trusting God More*; *Acts: Awakening to God in Everyday Life*; *The Names of God: His Character Revealed*; *Romans: Good News that Changes Everything*; *Elijah: Spiritual Stamina in Every Season*; *Numbers: Learning Contentment in a Culture of More*; *First Corinthians: Living Love When We Disagree*; *Joseph: The Journey to Forgiveness*; and *Jeremiah: Daring to Hope in an Unstable World*. She has also authored several books, including *Dare to Hope*; *Total Family Makeover: 8 Practical Steps to Making Disciples at Home*; and *Total Christmas Makeover: 31 Devotions to Celebrate with Purpose*. She is a regular contributor to the Proverbs 31 First Five App. Melissa lives in Waxahachie, Texas, with her pastor husband, Sean, and has four grown children: Zach, Abby, Sara, and Rachel.

FOLLOW MELISSA

Twitter	@MelSpoelstra
Instagram	@Melissa.Spoelstra
Facebook	/AuthorMelissaSpoelstra
Website	MelissaSpoelstra.com

AM-Praise
noon - Asking For -care/prayer
P. M- thank you for

H.S please give me a fresh understands
Gospel = greatest news of all times

John 5:24
memory verse

memory
John 1:12
verse

John 7:22 memory
verse

John 14:27 ✱

SESSION
ONE

Philippians 4:6-7

Praise God Before get out of bed

John 21

Introduction

TO THIS STUDY

do / Pray
every day Ask
Thanks

Mom's Meditation t

Four of my immediate five family members are more than six feet tall. When our family is walking together, I often have to request a slower pace because I can't keep up with my tall tribe. I don't want to miss the conversation. I want to move at their pace so I can soak up their presence.

While I desire a close relationship with my family, I find the one running ahead in my relationship with God is often me. I can get moving pretty fast answering emails, making appointments, and checking off my to-do list. What about you? Is something preventing you from lingering with Jesus lately?

In the pages of the Gospel of John, we can slow down and savor the peace of Jesus in a chaotic world. When we look at the pace of Jesus during His early life and ministry, we realize the need to slow down and soak up His presence. Yet, in our culture teeming with noise, screens, and busy schedules, we can fail to embrace the gift of peace Jesus promised. I often find myself worried about yesterday's problems and fearful of future ones. I don't want to give chaos authority in my life when Jesus offers me peace—but I wonder what it looks like to embrace His gift in the midst of a hectic life.

Savioring

Challenge for the whole study

Jesus warned us that the world cannot give the kind of peace of heart and mind He spoke about (John 14:27). This peace involves stillness of soul rather than circumstantial ease. In fact, the Greek word used in John's Gospel for "peace" is *eirene*, which is "the tranquil state of a soul assured of its salvation through Christ, and so fearing nothing from God and content with its earthly lot, of whatsoever sort that is."[1] But how do we receive this gift of peace? No exotic vacation, day at the spa, or Uber Eats® delivery can supply it.

Sometimes I think peace will appear when troubles disappear—when the house is clean, the car is fixed, the surgery is over, and so forth. Yet, Jesus doesn't define *peace* this way. He says we can have peace—that tranquil state of the soul—in the midst of the trials and difficulties we have in this world. Does that sound good to anyone else? Then I hope you'll meet me in the pages of John!

In this seven session Bible study in the Gospel of John, we will slow down to savor our relationship with Jesus. We won't just study Him—but spend time with Him and personally respond to what we are reading. Throughout the pages of the fourth Gospel, we will discover peace in the plan (1–3), power (4–6), patience (7–9), purposes (10–13), promises (14–17), and passion (18–21) of Jesus.

One of the things I love about John's Gospel is that he wrote it at the end of his life. We'll find editorial comments throughout his account helping us see what the disciples understood much more fully in the decades after Jesus left the earth. The Gospel of John was written much later than the Synoptic Gospels—Matthew, Mark, and Luke. They are referred to as synoptic because they contain a high percentage of overlapping content. John contains more than ninety percent unique material, recording stories, miracles, and details not found in the other Gospels.[2]

Omitting the formal teachings of Jesus, like the Sermon on the Mount and transfiguration, John's Gospel traces the informal relationship of Jesus to His disciples. As we turn John's pages, we'll take the posture of a learner—seeking to glean all that we can from Jesus's message and methods. At the end of each day of study, we'll take time for a Stop and Savor section to ask questions like, *What did Jesus say?* and *What did Jesus do?*

To explore how John's Gospel is set apart from Matthew, Mark, and Luke, check out the Digging Deeper article "John and the Synoptics" found online at **lifeway.com/gospelofjohn.**

Throughout our study we'll find mentions of the Jewish festivals, which were holy days meant for slowing down and remembering what God had done in the past. Our entire study will incorporate this concept of deceleration to appreciate the pace of our Savior. He never hurried, but completed all that the Father called Him to accomplish.

We will take a fresh look at Jesus's life and ministry so that we might grow in intimacy with Him. Together we will sit at a wedding in Cana, witness miraculous healings and feedings, and meet individuals of all different backgrounds who discovered peace in their own chaos by believing in Jesus.

John explicitly told us why he penned these pages. His goal was for people to believe in Jesus and that by believing they would have life in His name. He was talking about abundant life—enjoying the gift of peace of mind and heart that Jesus freely offers.

OPTIONS FOR STUDY

Any time we begin a new Bible study, it's important to set realistic expectations for ourselves based on our current season of life. I know in some seasons we have extra time for more in-depth study, Scripture memory work, and additional reading. Other times—such as when our faith is new, our schedule is packed, or our children are small—we don't want to bite off more than we can chew and feel frustrated for not meeting our goals. As we study the Gospel of John together, I hope you'll choose a study method that is realistic for you but also challenges you to grow in your spiritual rhythms. Consider the following options and prayerfully decide what will be the right fit for your current season and situation.

1. **BASIC STUDY.** The basic study includes five days of content that combine study of Scripture with personal reflection and application. This includes looking up Scripture, reflecting, engaging in interactive activities, and answering questions. At the end of each day, you'll find a Stop and Savor portion featuring reflection questions and a prayer.

2. **IN-DEPTH STUDY.** If you feel up to more study, here are a few ideas
I recommend:

- **WATCH** the teaching videos that accompany each session. You have
  access to video teaching that provides additional content to help you
  better understand and apply what you just studied in the previous session.
  You'll find detailed information for how to access the teaching videos that
  accompany this study in the back of your Bible study book. You'll also find
  a Viewer Guide page at the end of each session, where you can follow along
  with the videos and take notes on the teaching.

- **DISCUSS** your study and the teaching videos with a group. If you're doing
  this study with a group, you can use the questions and prompts provided on
  the Group Session pages to help you review the previous five days of study
  and discuss the video teaching together.

- **MEMORIZE** the weekly Bible verses. It is helpful to recite these verses with a
  partner, so find a friend in your group who is also choosing an in-depth option.

- **READ** the Digging Deeper articles available online (**lifeway.com/gospelofjohn**)
  for deeper exploration of the text and themes. There's also a reading plan for
  the Gospel of John on page 180 to mark your progress throughout the study.

- **ADD** to your study by using a study Bible or any of these free commentaries:
  studylight.org/commentaries
  biblestudytools.com/commentaries
  biblegateway.com/resources/commentaries
  biblehub.com/commentaries
  blueletterbible.org/study.cfm

3. **KEEPING IT SIMPLE.** Depending on your circumstances, you may want
to modify your goals. Perhaps it will be a win if you attend group meetings,
complete three out of five days of your study, or make some other modification
to your plan. Our desire is not to check boxes but to savor the peace of Jesus in
our own lives. Pray for guidance, and set your goal accordingly.

Take time now to decide which study option feels right for you, and check it below.

___ **1. Basic Study**
___ **2. In-Depth Study**
___ **3. Keeping It Simple: I will** _____.

Be sure to let someone in your group know which option you have chosen so that you
have some accountability and encouragement.

A NOTE FOR GROUP LEADERS

If you are leading a Bible study group through *The Gospel of John,* then first I want to say thank you! I have no doubt God will use you to encourage the women in your group as you walk through His Word together. In addition to the teaching videos, here are a few resources to aid you as you facilitate your group:

- **DISCUSSION QUESTIONS** are found on the Group Discussion Guide pages at the end of each week of study.

- **TEACHING VIDEOS** to watch at each group session. You'll find detailed information for how to access the teaching videos that accompany this study in the back of your Bible study book. At your first group meeting, watch the Session One video together, discuss the questions provided, and make sure all the women in your group have their Bible study book. When you gather for Session Two, you'll discuss what you studied during the week and then watch the Session Two teaching video together.

- **A LEADER VIDEO** and a leader guide are available for free at **lifeway.com/gospelofjohn.**

- Also don't miss the **FREE CHURCH PROMOTIONAL RESOURCES** found at **lifeway.com/gospelofjohn**—including a PowerPoint® template, promotional poster, and bulletin insert—to help you promote the study in your church or neighborhood.

A FINAL WORD

I can't wait to get started on this journey alongside you. I'm excited to slow down and linger with Jesus to receive the gift of peace He promised. I pray you'll join me in the pages of John's Gospel, and we can grow in our faith, find life, and savor peace together.

SESSION ONE

Video Viewer Guide

Chaos around us often can _create_ chaos within us.

Gospel of John background information:

- John contains _90_ % unique content from the other Gospels.

- John wrote his Gospel in his _old_ _age_ .

- The original audience of John's Gospel was likely
  Jewish .

Peace is a _Person_ .

We need a fresh look at Jesus so the familiar doesn't fade our
fasination with Him.

"Don't worry about anything; instead, _pray_ about everything.
Tell God what you need, and thank him for all he has done."
PHILIPPIANS 4:6, NLT

ACTION STEP: Use this acronym (based on Philippians 4:6) in prayer
over the course of our study.

Morning: P _Praise_

Afternoon: A _Ask_

Evening: T _hanks_

(Answers are available on p. 185.)

GROUP DISCUSSION GUIDE

LEADER: Before your first meeting, watch the Leader Video posted at lifeway.com/gospelofjohn. Use this guide to facilitate your group meeting. If your group members are watching the videos on their own, rather than together during your gathering, you'll want to select two or three questions from the days of personal study to add to your discussion time.

SHARE: Guide each group member to share her name and her favorite ice cream flavor.

WATCH the video "Session One: Savoring the Peace of Jesus in a Chaotic World" together and follow along with the viewer guide on the previous page.

VIDEO DISCUSSION

1. *Discuss:* From the background information in the introductory video, what is something new or something that caught your attention about the Gospel of John?

2. Turn in your Bibles to the following verses and ask volunteers to read them out loud: John 1:12; 5:24; 7:24; 10:10; 14:27; 20:31; and Philippians 4:6. Encourage participants to share what stood out to them from these passages.

STUDY DISCUSSION

1. *Ask:* How does savoring the peace of Jesus resonate in your life today?

2. Turn to page 7 and read aloud the section titled, "Options for Study." Give women time to consider which level of study they will choose. Then ask women to share which option they marked.

3. *Ask:* What is something you are looking forward to or hoping to learn as we begin studying the Gospel of John?

REVIEW: Remind your group to complete the five days of personal study for "Session Two: Savoring Peace in the Plan of Jesus." Take a moment to highlight the Big Idea for each day. These key points will be important to review at the end of the week of study.

PRAYER: Close your group meeting with a time of prayer.* Depending on the size of your group, consider breaking into smaller groups of two or three women and praying for each other. You might have extra time since this is the introductory week.

*Be sure to watch the leader video found at lifeway.com/gospelofjohn for some ideas for varying your prayer time together.

 To access the video teaching sessions, use the instructions in the back of your Bible study book.

SESSION
TWO

PEACE IN THE

PLAN

OF JESUS

BUT TO ALL WHO BELIEVED
HIM AND ACCEPTED HIM,
HE GAVE THE RIGHT TO
BECOME CHILDREN OF GOD.

John 1:12

Day One

A PRE-EXISTING PLAN

SCRIPTURE FOCUS

John 1:1-34

BIG IDEA

Circumstances can feel confusing, but we can savor peace knowing that God established a plan before the beginning of time.

I searched everywhere, but I could not find my car key. I mentally retraced my steps and deduced that I must have locked it in the car. My helper husband attempted to get into the vehicle using a wire coat hanger with no success except to leave some permanent scratches. I then called a locksmith who charged a healthy sum to open the car door. Once inside, we discovered the key was nowhere to be found. Eventually, we found it on the bathroom floor. I'd like to tell you this all happened calmly with no worry, hurry, or frustration. But that's not how it went down. At the end of the incident, I reflected on how pointless the whole situation seemed— damage done, money spent, and nothing to show for it.

Have you encountered similar situations? If so, jot a few sentences about your experience. But why worry- ~~I al~~ ~~and~~ ~~mistakes happen~~ first-rest Duplex - Water leak from the house. Upset more maintenance. It cost us a couple thousand. A couple of months later I went thru insurance + we had coverage.

Trying to make sense of small frustrations like lost keys or more significant issues like physical pain, financial loss, or relational strain can rob us of peace. As we open the pages of the Gospel of John, we remember life is not random. Despite confusing circumstances, we can savor peace, knowing that God established a plan before the beginning of time. He is "always working" (John 5:17). Even when we don't feel it or see it, we can believe it.

Life is a key theme in John's Gospel. He uses the Greek word for "life," zoe, thirty-six times.[1]

THE WORD

Matthew began his Gospel with a genealogy connecting Joseph to Abraham, and Luke recorded the lineage of Jesus, tracing Mary's family tree to Adam. John reached back even further to Jesus's role in creation.

READ JOHN 1:1-5 and answer the following questions:

Who is "the Word" John referred to and what do we find out about Him in these verses?

"The Word" = Jesus - he was created before time. In the beginning was the word, + the word was with God, and the word was God. Thru Him all things were made. In him was life. The light was the light of man.

**In your own words, summarize what is stated or
implied about the Word's relationship to God,
His existence, and His work.**

*Jesus/God/Hs are 3 in 1 God. Jesus was the
Son of God, and God did creative works ! God
Jesus existence was from God His work was to save the
sinners & the poor*

John wrote in
Revelation that
Jesus is "Alpha" and
"Omega"—the first
and last letters of
the Greek alphabet.
(Rev. 1:8; 22:13).
This was a definitive
statement about
Christ's eternality.
He sees and knows
the beginning
and the end.

The Greek word *Logos* labeling Jesus as the Word was used exclusively
by John. His opening words are reminiscent of the book of Genesis and
reveal the Son of God's role in creation. The Father accomplished His
creative work through the Son (Col. 1:16; Heb. 1:2). John's wording also
makes a statement about Jesus's eternal existence. He was not created, nor
born. There has never been a time when He did not exist in community
with the Father and the Holy Spirit. *Well he was born thru Mary who
was made in their body*

Jesus being referred to as the Word (*Logos*) indicates words matter. Author
Rosario Butterfield referenced this passage when she wrote, "When we change
the language, we change the logic. We want to frame our understanding of life
through the lens of the Word made flesh—the One who gives life and light."[2]

**Take a moment to consider how you're currently living
out God's purpose in your life. Write a short prayer
asking God for peace as you begin this study.**

*Lord This question of my purpose—what is my purpose?
God I need to be able to live a life that values all
the love you give me. I am asking you from my heart—
please help me relax in your love. My mind is constantly spinning
and I can't focus on any one thing. I need rest in peace with
you at my side. What is my purpose & I need to know why am I always
in a daze please guide me to the place you want me to be.*

DWELT AMONG US

**The deeper we know Jesus, the more we experience
peace in His plan. READ JOHN 1:6-18 and record
what Jesus did according to verse 14.**

The Word "became human and made his home among us" (v. 14).
Theologians refer to this action as the Incarnation. The verb used for
"made his home" means "to pitch a tent, to dwell temporarily."[3] Jesus

existed before creation but stepped into time and became one of us. He temporarily tabernacled among us on earth to live the perfect life we couldn't live and ultimately die on our behalf as the atoning sacrifice.

God put on flesh and came to earth to restore our broken relationship with Him. He came near.

Take a moment to savor His nearness. Fill in the blanks:

Jesus came to earth for _____ (your name) and is near in the midst of _____ (a challenging circumstance) in my life.

THE LAMB OF GOD

Jesus is the Word, the Life, the Light, and filled with grace and truth. His plan to redeem us meant He would lay down His life in exchange for ours.

READ JOHN 1:19-34 and summarize how John the Baptist described Jesus in the verses below:

Verse 29

Verse 30

Verse 34

John the Baptist and John, the author of this Gospel, are different individuals. John the Baptist was Jesus's cousin whose ministry preceded and prepared the way according to God's plan. John the author was the son of Zebedee and brother of James.

From the beginning of Jesus's ministry, John the Baptist called Him the Lamb of God. The first readers of John's Gospel would have been familiar with the use of lambs for Jewish sacrifices, as commanded in the Old Testament. Each family had to have one for Passover (Ex. 12:1-10). When John the Baptist spoke this title over Jesus, he was foreshadowing Christ's sacrificial death to pay the penalty for my sin and yours.

Take a moment to reflect on the price Jesus paid on your behalf and thank Him for the right He has given you to become a child of God by believing in His name (John 1:12). Remember, no one is physically born a child of God. It happens by grace through faith (Eph. 2:1-10).

If you've placed your faith in Christ, share about your experience. If you're not yet a follower of Christ, see page 181 for information on making that decision.

Whether your commitment to Christ began last week or decades ago, we all have days when ambiguity creeps into our complicated lives. Some moments may feel pointless and frustrating. Others filled with tumultuous circumstances threaten our peace with much greater force. Regardless, we can hold onto God's peace because He isn't stumbling through His calendar. His plan was conceived before time began—and that plan includes intimacy with Him!

As we walk through this study, we want to grow in experiencing God's peace. To help us do that, we'll wrap up each day by savoring what God revealed through John's Gospel about Jesus.

STOP AND SAVOR

Today we focused on this truth: *Circumstances can feel confusing, but we can savor peace knowing that God established a plan before the beginning of time.*

Summarize your personal takeaway from today's lesson.

As you reflect on today's passage, record a few words or phrases about Jesus that stood out to you.

Consider your life circumstances and complete the following sentence:

Because Jesus is Creator, the Word, Life, Light, full of grace and truth, and the Lamb of God who takes away my sin, I can experience peace in _____ _____.

PRAYER

Lord, thank You for revealing Your Son to me through John's Gospel. When my plans are frustrated, help me to lean into Yours. Give me eyes to see where You are at work all around me. You are my Creator, my Life, my Light, the Living Word, and I'm so grateful that You are the Lamb of God who takes away my sin. Align my plans to Your grace and truth today, and give me Your peace. In Jesus's name, Amen.

Day Two
COME AND SEE

SCRIPTURE
FOCUS
John 1:35-51

BIG IDEA

We can savor peace when we respond to Jesus's invitation to come and see.

At restaurants I am often the first person at the table to decide what I want. As soon as I identify something that sounds good, I stop looking at the other choices. While this saves me from analysis paralysis, it also means I sometimes make hasty decisions.

Following Jesus means slowing down and considering our actions and decisions in light of His plan. We can't afford to choose our morality or devotion from the world's menu. Instead, we need to accept Jesus's invitation for us to come and see His plan for living.

WHAT DO YOU WANT?

The first followers of Jesus came to Him through the ministry of His cousin, John the Baptist.

READ JOHN 1:35-39 and draw a line to the person who said each statement:

"Look! There is the Lamb of God!" (v. 36).   Jesus

"What do you want?" (v. 38).
                                                          John's two disciples
"Rabbi, . . . where are you staying?" (v. 38).

"Come and see" (v. 39).   John the Baptist

What stands out to you from this dialogue?

It's interesting that Jesus started the conversation by asking the two men following Him what they wanted. I mean, He's God—He knows everything. But His question helped them clarify their desires. They weren't looking for an address when they responded by asking where Jesus was staying. They called Him "Rabbi," which was a term of respect given to Jewish teachers that literally means, "Master."[4] Embedded in their question was a desire to be with Jesus and listen to His message.

Jesus didn't give them a detailed sermon about His incarnation. Instead, He invited them to "come and see"—not just so they could check out His lodging, but to spend time with Him. He extends the same invitation to us, to be in a relationship with Him. We do that through the power of His Spirit, by obeying His Word, and in community with His people. He leads us as we make a myriad of decisions about our thoughts, attitudes, words, and actions. Understanding His purpose, instead of just leaning on our own understanding, helps us make sense of our circumstances.

> Take a moment to respond to the words of Jesus from this passage. How do they resonate in your life?

> *What do you want?*

> *Come and see.*

RESPONDING TO JESUS

> READ JOHN 1:40-51 and record information given about the following people:

> Andrew (vv. 40-42,44)

> Peter (vv. 40-42,44)

Like Andrew and Peter, Philip was from Galilee and likely a fisherman. His hometown of Bethsaida literally means "house of fishing."[5]

Philip (vv. 43-45)

Nathanael (vv. 45-49)

What are some patterns or repeated phrases in the text?

Once people discovered Jesus, they wanted to bring their friends and relatives to Him. Philip even used Jesus's words in answering Nathanael's objections: "come and see."

Jesus didn't start His ministry with a big tent revival. He called individuals who then told others, who in turn told more people. Scholars surmise Nathanael was a student of Jewish law since Philip appealed to him by referencing Moses and the prophets. Jesus seemed to confirm that by stating He saw Nathanael under the fig tree. The fig tree phrase was used in rabbinic literature to describe meditation on the law.[6] In verse 51, Jesus referred to Jacob's vision of seeing a ladder (Gen. 28:10-17). He knew Nathanael, as a student of the Scriptures, was familiar with the story. Jesus was pointing to Himself as that stairway—the mediator between God and man.

Jesus didn't rush to accomplish His plan, revealing a portion at a time. He responded to seekers and sought out others, inviting them to come and see.

COME AND SEE

When it comes to following Jesus, we often want the whole plan laid out. Yet Jesus just says "Come and see." He invites us into a deeper relationship—to know Him and learn from Him. Often, His words prompt me to respond similarly to King David's words in Psalm 27:8: "My heart has heard you say, 'Come and talk with me.' And my heart responds, 'LORD, I am coming.'" Other times my heart responds, but not with an eagerness to join Him. I'm busy, distracted, or overwhelmed.

What are some ways you might fill in this blank:

My heart responds, Lord, I am _____.

Today, I've intentionally left some extra time to respond like King David. Use the next few minutes to think about Jesus's invitation to follow Him. Consider the following questions. Feel free to write responses or just think through them silently:

What helps you follow Jesus more closely?

What hinders you from following Him?

Where have you been too focused on your own plans?

How would your day be different if you consistently and intentionally sought the plan of Jesus?

Is there anyone the Lord is prompting you to invite to "come and see"?

Now take some time to envision Jesus as the stairway between you and God. Write a prayer below, thanking Christ for being your mediator and asking Him to help you connect with Him more intimately through our study of the Gospel of John.

STOP AND SAVOR

Today we focused on this truth: *We can savor peace when we respond to Jesus's invitation to come and see.*

Summarize your personal takeaway from today's lesson.

What did you notice about the plan and pace of Jesus in this passage?

How are you responding to Jesus's invitation to come and see?

Day Three

DO WHAT HE SAYS

As a pastor, my husband has officiated many weddings where things went wrong. Once he forgot to have the audience sit down, and they stood for the entire ceremony. Another time, a truck ran over the water main at the reception hall, leaving them with no water at the reception. These examples reveal that no matter how much you plan, unexpected things can and will happen!

I wonder if you have attended a wedding or other special event where something went wrong. If something comes to mind, jot it below.

SCRIPTURE FOCUS
John 2:1-22

BIG IDEA
If we desire the peace of Jesus, then we must do what He says.

THE PROBLEM

READ JOHN 2:1-3 and describe the problem that surfaced at the wedding in Cana.

Cana was about nine miles north of Nazareth where Jesus grew up, so it's possible His mother was a friend of the wedding family. Since there is no mention of Joseph, many scholars believe he had already died.[9]

Running out of food or beverages at a wedding today would be embarrassing for the hosts. In biblical times, it was catastrophic. A groom could face a lawsuit over this lapse in hospitality.[7] And this kind of social embarrassment could have been joked about by people in their community for years.[8] I love how Mary chose to get involved, bringing the situation to Jesus.

I usually seek logical solutions in difficult situations. Often, I'll call a friend or mentor for advice. Other times I look to Google® or YouTube® for answers.

What are some ways you typically approach problems?

Like Mary, we need to bring the sticky situations we encounter directly to Jesus.

THE PLAN

READ JOHN 2:4-12 and answer the following questions:

What was Jesus's initial response to His mother's plea?

How did Mary instruct the servants?

What did Jesus reveal for the first time at this event (v. 11)?

While the other Gospel writers recorded more than forty miracles, John chose only seven to highlight. He referred to them as signs because they pointed to something significant.

Jesus referring to His mom as "woman" (v. 4) sounds almost rude through our cultural filters. But in His day this was a title of respect—like saying ma'am or madam.[10] Mary was His earthly mother, but He was shifting into public ministry and to His heavenly Father's business.

Jesus's response to Mary that His hour had not yet come is interesting. In ancient sources, one's hour or time referred to one's death. Scholar Craig Keener wrote, "Jesus may be saying, 'Once I begin performing signs, I start toward the cross.'"[11]

Even though Jesus initially pushed back, He did perform His first miracle, or sign, as John called it. This act has less application in debates about alcoholic beverages and more to teach us about Jesus's identity. He revealed His glory.

What stands out to you as significant in this passage?

You may have written any number of things, but I noticed that Jesus's first miracle recorded in John was high in quantity and quality. Each of the six stone jars filled with water for ritual cleansing held twenty to thirty gallons. So Jesus made up to 180 gallons of wine. Most commentators agree that "this large amount is a sign of the abundance of God's grace."[12] To use the stone jars for wine would have violated custom, but Jesus valued people over customs. Also note that Jesus replaced Old Testament law (water for ceremonial cleansing) with abundant grace (high quality wine) ultimately pictured in the communion supper where wine represents His blood.

Jesus brought fullness where there was emptiness and joy where there was disappointment. He longs to do that in our lives as well.

Are emptiness and disappointment words that describe your current circumstances? If so, explain.

The first step to discovering the fullness and joy evidenced in Jesus's first sign is to do what He says. Obedience places us on the path to God's peace.

Where has God's Word been nudging you toward obedience? Make a few notes below.

Moses's first miracle turned water into blood, which was a plague of judgment. Jesus's first miracle recorded in John turned water into wine, which was a blessing of grace.

Moses's final plague was the death of firstborn sons. Jesus's final sign in John's Gospel is the raising of Lazarus.

For additional insights into Jewish weddings and funerals during the time of Jesus, check out the Digging Deeper article "Weddings and Funerals" found online at lifeway.com/gospelofjohn.

The Synoptic Gospels (Matthew, Mark, Luke) placed the cleansing of the temple much closer to Jesus's death chronologically, whereas John set it at the beginning of His ministry. Scholars suggest that either Jesus cleared the temple twice or, in the practice of ancient biography, John rearranged the sequence to clarify his teaching point.[13]

John established Jesus's divinity in the beginning of this Gospel and now shows us His glory. Jesus's disciples believed in Him. We can choose to do the same. If we want God's peace, then we must live according to His plan.

THE PASSION

Once Jesus began His ministry, He traveled from Galilee to Jerusalem to celebrate the Passover with His disciples. There He continued to reveal Himself as the Son of God.

> READ JOHN 2:13-22 and record the order of Jesus's actions (1 through 6):
>
> ___ Poured out (or scattered) coins on the floor
>
> ___ Made a whip (or scourge)
>
> ___ Drove out everyone with sheep and cattle
>
> ___ Turned over tables
>
> ___ Told them to stop turning His Father's House into a marketplace (or house of trade, business, merchandise, market)
>
> ___ Chased out money changers
>
> What statement was Jesus making with His actions in the temple courts?

Jesus offers us abundant grace but desires His people to follow the Father's plan. In Jesus's day, that didn't include using the temple for profit. The condition of the temple was a vivid indication of the spiritual condition of the nation. The people were manipulating religion for money. Jesus knew there was no peace to be found in that practice, then or now.

He spoke boldly about abuses. The religious leaders asked for a sign. Jesus responded with prophetic words about destroying the temple and rebuilding it in three days. This confounded the leaders because Herod's temple, which was started in 20 BC, was not completed at the time of this encounter. However, Jesus wasn't talking about a building, but His body. This kind of misunderstanding of spiritual truth, where hearers misinterpreted Jesus's words, is found throughout John's Gospel.[14]

Jesus is full of grace, but also full of truth. Peace in following Him is not always found in the path of least resistance. Sometimes doing what He says means doing hard things.

STOP AND SAVOR

Today we focused on this truth: *If we desire the peace of Jesus, then we must do what He says.*

Summarize your personal takeaway from today's lesson.

What stood out to you from Jesus's words and actions?

How have you noticed a connection between obedience and peace in your life?

Day Four

YOU MUST BE BORN AGAIN

SCRIPTURE FOCUS

John 2:23–3:21

My first child made his appearance into the world eight days after my expected due date. After Zach was delivered, I reflected in awe on the process of labor that every mother goes through to deliver her baby. I was overwhelmed by it.

What stories regarding a baby coming into the world stand out to you?

BIG IDEA

Jesus makes a distinction between sincere and superficial belief.

SINCERE BELIEF

In our study of John today, Jesus will discuss the process of spiritual birth with a seeker.

READ JOHN 2:23-25 to set the stage for that conversation. Describe what you discover about Jesus.

The Greek word translated "believed" or "trusted" is *pisteuo,* which means "to think to be true, to be persuaded of, to credit, place confidence in."[15] We will encounter this word eighty-five times in the book of John.[16]

Our English translations sometimes miss the play on words used in the original Greek. In John 2:23, Jesus essentially said some people believed in Him, but He didn't believe in them. What we discover in this passage is that belief can be superficial. Jesus knew those who had sincere belief and those just momentarily awed by miracles.

Signs could be the place where faith starts. John recorded miracles in his Gospel for that purpose (John 20:30-31). But genuine belief was necessary for spiritual rebirth. Attractional activities that pique an interest in the gospel message aren't bad, they just aren't enough. A person must move from superficial to sincere belief. Jesus revealed in these verses that people who want to experience His works without submitting to His Word will not share His life.

BORN AGAIN

One man who saw Jesus's miraculous signs wasn't easily convinced; he asked questions to delve deeper into Jesus's teaching.

READ JOHN 3:1-12 and record the questions Nicodemus asked.

VERSE 4	VERSE 9

Nicodemus belonged to a group called the Pharisees whose focus was strict obedience to the law. He also was one of the seventy-one members of the Sanhedrin. Nicodemus approached Jesus using the term of respect —*Rabbi*—assuming Jesus was a teacher who came from God. What he didn't realize was that He was God who had come to teach!

Scholars have debated why Nicodemus came to Jesus at night. What might be a possible reason?

The Sanhedrin functioned as a Jewish governing body who made laws and enforced them. Imagine the supreme court and senate rolled into one.

Since the text doesn't tell us, we can only speculate.

- *Perhaps he feared what colleagues might think of him and didn't want to be seen with Jesus.*

- *Maybe he wanted undisturbed time with Jesus away from the crowd.*

- *As one with ruling authority, he might have been busy during the day with pressing responsibilities.*

Regardless of the reason for this encounter, we can find an application for our own lives. Public worship and study gatherings are important, but there are things we can't get from Jesus with the crowd. We need personal, intimate meetings with our Savior.

What spiritual rhythms have you established for private meetings with Jesus?

How do you think your life would be different if you had more personal time with the Lord each day?

Nicodemus acknowledged the signs Jesus performed but struggled with Jesus's teaching regarding spiritual rebirth. He couldn't move what Jesus was saying out of the realm of physical birth: "How can an old man go back into his mother's womb and be born again?" (v. 4). But Jesus stated this was a different kind of birth, one "of water and the Spirit" (v. 5).

What do you think He meant by water and Spirit?

Scholars do not agree on the exact meaning of Jesus's statement regarding water and Spirit. Some have latched onto this statement to assert baptism as a requirement for salvation. Water baptism is an important step of obedience for a Christian, but Jesus wasn't referencing it directly in this conversation. Some say both elements, water and spirit, point to a picture of life and together they refer to spiritual birth. Others say being "born of water" references physical birth, as during childbirth, a mother's amniotic sac breaks, releasing a watery substance. I lean toward this interpretation. So, Jesus was saying a person can't enter the kingdom of God without being born physically (water) and spiritually (Spirit).

Using the birth analogy, Jesus revealed that just as you cannot manufacture babies, you cannot manufacture Christians.[17] Yes, spiritual birth is a mystery, but it is necessary and observable. Jesus used the wind to illustrate. You don't know the origin of the wind, but its effects are evident. In the same way, spiritual birth can't be seen, but the transformation is unmistakable.

If you have experienced spiritual birth as Jesus described, what's been the effect on your life?

Spiritual birth occurs at the moment of sincere belief. I believed in Jesus when I was nine years old. The transformation wasn't hugely evident in the following days and months, but over the course of forty years the wind of God's Spirit has altered everything.

Jesus made a play on words in the Greek. *Wind* is *pneuma* in Greek, which "can mean *wind*, *breath*, or *spirit*. He said, 'You have to be born of the Spirit, and it's like the wind.' In other words, the *pneuma* is like the *pneuma*."[18]

LIFTED UP

READ JOHN 3:13-21 and record below the benefits associated with belief in these verses.

VERSE 15	VERSE 16	VERSE 18

"Lifting up" is a term used in Scripture for both "exaltation and execution."[19]

Those who believe in Jesus ("the Son") receive eternal life and have no judgment against them, because Jesus came not to condemn but to save. This is good news!

Jesus foreshadowed how salvation would be accomplished with an Old Testament reference. In Numbers 21:4-9, the Lord sent poisonous snakes among the people of Israel because of their complaining. Many people were bitten and died. When Moses interceded for the people, God instructed him to make a bronze replica of a snake and attach it to a pole. The people were to look at it to be healed.

As the snake replica was lifted up on a pole and the Israelites found healing, Jesus would be lifted up on a cross so we could, by faith, find salvation in Him. As pastor R. C. Sproul said, "It is the good news that snake-bitten people, people infected by a poison that goes to the depth of their souls, can look to the cross and find salvation."[20]

Jesus used several illustrations to help explain salvation—birth, wind, the serpent on a pole, light and darkness. Which is the most helpful to you in wrapping your mind around what it means to be a Christian?

God loved us so much He sent Jesus to save us from sin. Yet we must believe in Him. This belief must move beyond a superficial longing for His works to a sincere faith that trusts His Word.

PRAYER

Jesus, thank You for giving Your life for mine. I long to come to You privately more often to work through my questions and doubts. Reveal Yourself to me and give me eyes to see the effects of Your spiritual wind around me. Thank You for loving me so much. I believe in You, Jesus. Help my faith to grow deeper. In Jesus's name, Amen.

STOP AND SAVOR

Today we focused on this truth: *Jesus makes a distinction between sincere and superficial belief.*

Summarize your personal takeaway from today's lesson.

What stood out to you about what Jesus said?

Meditate for a moment about eternal life—living forever with Jesus. Savor this gift as it relates to your past, present, and future.

Day Five

HE MUST INCREASE

When some friends left our church, I took it way too personally. Even though I knew they had prayed about it and had good reasons to leave, it stung. They had attended the small group led by my husband and me. *Were we not enough? What did they find more appealing about their new church? Why hadn't they shared their concerns about our church with us?* Others in the group wanted to "process" our mutual friends' exit as well. The temptation for gossip and self-protection presented itself often over the coming days and weeks.

Can you relate to the struggle that takes place when someone leaves your church or ministry? If so, jot some thoughts about it below.

SCRIPTURE FOCUS
John 3:22-36

BIG IDEA
Seek God-connection over self-protection.

I've heard it said that there is no pain like church pain. When any sort of ministry conflict arises, self-protection is my default. I want to defend my position, shield my reputation, and rally people to my side. However, John the Baptist showed us another way. He revealed that peace comes in following God's plan.

SEE OURSELVES CLEARLY

READ JOHN 3:22-30 and circle the letter that best answers the following questions:

What were both Jesus and John the Baptist doing?

    A. Sleeping

    B. Baptizing

    C. Healing

Warren Wiersbe noted that four prominent men in the Bible addressed the problem of comparison and competition: Moses (Num. 11:26-30), John the Baptist (John 3:26-30), Jesus (Luke 9:46-50), and Paul (Phil. 1:15-18). Wiersbe stated: "A leader often suffers more from his zealous disciples than from his critics!"[21]

What did John the Baptist's disciples complain about?

A. The Jew who debated with them over ceremonial cleansing

B. The temperature of the baptismal waters

C. People leaving their ministry for another

How did John the Baptist respond to their complaints?

A. No one receives anything unless God gives it.

B. I have told you plainly I am not the Messiah.

C. Jesus must increase, and I must decrease.

D. All of the above.

In college, I wrote a paper on C. S. Lewis's novel, *Till We Have Faces*. The main character Orual struggled with insecurity and jealousy, which caused her to hate the supernatural. My thesis for the paper has stuck with me over three decades: "Sometimes we tell lies about ourselves that cause us to tell lies about God." Consider the following questions in light of that truth:

How did John the Baptist see himself according to these verses?

How did he see Jesus?

John the Baptist gave an honest assessment. He didn't discount his ministry or purpose; he leaned into his high calling from God to prepare the way for Jesus. For a season this meant greater visibility and recognition. However, he trusted God's plan—realizing the time had come for a decrease in his baptisms, preaching, and popularity. Commentator D. A. Carson said, "Both John and Jesus were given their roles by heaven (v. 27), and John was entirely content with his."[22] When we see ourselves clearly, we will be content with God's plan for our lives and express genuine joy for the success of others.

(Answers: B, A, D)

Take a few minutes to reflect and thoughtfully answer the questions below:

How is this message landing in your soul today? Can you identify any lies you might be telling yourself?

What does it mean for Christ to increase and you to decrease? Where is this needing to happen in your life?

Are you content in your current calling? Are you able to celebrate the success of others in similar roles? Explain.

John the Baptist's words remind me that I have blind spots. I need to see myself clearly so that I can see God more clearly. This means I take time to reflect, ask the Lord to reveal weaknesses, and give trusted friends permission to speak corrective words when needed.

KEEP THE CHATTER VERTICAL

Scholars are uncertain who is speaking the words in verses 31-36. It could be Jesus, John the Gospel writer, or John the Baptist. I tend to see this as John the Baptist. I believe he kept the chatter vertical by pointing to Jesus.

READ JOHN 3:31-35 and record below any words or phrases used to describe Jesus.

Here are some that stood out to me:

- Greater than anyone else
- Testifies about what He has seen and heard

- Speaks God's words
- Given the Spirit without limit
- Loved by the Father

Rather than strategize attractional ways to win back the crowd, John the Baptist made Jesus the focus of discussion. His heart was for his followers to be followers of Jesus.

John the Baptist highlighted the eternal plan above earthly priorities. This resonates strongly with me because I constantly get caught up in the stuff of earth—emails to answer, projects to finish, dishes to wash.

What earthly stuff has been consuming your focus lately?

Those things matter, but they aren't primary. What's challenging is helping friends caught up in temporal pursuits. I want to keep the chatter vertical to help them see beyond horizontal implications, but there's tension here. How do I listen to people's concerns, validate their feelings, yet at the same time point them toward God without seeming preachy or hyper-spiritual?

What are practical ways you have directed a conversation toward God in these situations?

I asked some godly women this question. Here are some of their ideas:
- Pray with the person right away.
- Be a listener and not a fixer.
- Redirect gossip or complaining with positive insights.
- Text a Bible verse or biblical principle God has used in your life.
- Ask good questions (like Jesus often did).

John's mention of the Holy Spirit in verse 34 reminds me that inviting the Spirit to guide us is another practical way to seek God-connection over self-protection in sticky situations.

How would our lives change if we talked to God first when problems arise in our marriages, friendships, families, and churches?

I experience more peace when I bring frustrations to the Lord. He also helps me work through emotions as I pray so I can respond rather than react to conflict. When our small group friends left the church, a wise advisor reminded my husband that we aren't competing for sheep. Instead, we ask the Lord to use us to seek and save the lost. That was a good encouragement to keep our focus on Jesus.

GOD CONNECTION

READ JOHN 3:36. What separates those who receive eternal life from those who receive eternal judgment?

Sincere belief in God's Son connects us to the Father. Jesus is the plan. We can savor peace when we savor Jesus.

STOP AND SAVOR

Today we focused on this truth: *Seek God-connection over self-protection.*

Summarize your personal takeaway from today's lesson.

What qualities of Jesus stood out to you in today's verses?

What do you need to apply from John the Baptist's testimony and teaching?

Video Viewer Guide

Our plans may fail, but we can savor peace in God's _____ plan.

God sent a _____ (John 1:1-5).

God set the _____ (John 1:14-18,29).

What are three things currently stealing your peace?

1.
2.
3.

When it comes to worry and concern, only one is _____.

Serenity Prayer: *God, grant me the serenity to accept the things I cannot change, courage to change the things I can, and the wisdom to know the difference, living one day at a time, enjoying one moment at a time; accepting hardship as a pathway to peace; taking, as Jesus did, this sinful world as it is not as I would have it. Trusting that You will make all things right if I surrender to Your will, that I might be reasonable happy in this world and supremely happy with You in the next.*

God loves the _____ (John 3:15-21).

God gets the _____.

CHALLENGE FOR THE WEEK: Pray at noon each day this week, asking God for peace for someone across the globe.

(Answers are available on p. 185.)

GROUP DISCUSSION GUIDE

SHARE: What are some plans coming up on your calendar, like parties, meetings, vacations, and so forth?

WATCH the video "Session Two: Savoring Peace in the Plan of Jesus" together and follow along with the viewer guide on the previous page.

MEMORY VERSE: Review John 1:12 and provide time for group members to recite it aloud.

VIDEO DISCUSSION
1. *Ask:* How did the Old Testament references in John 1 give you additional insight into John's Prologue?
2. *Discuss:* How does reviewing God's plan in John 1–3 bring you peace today? Share practical examples from your own life.

STUDY DISCUSSION
1. Encourage participants to share responses from their answers to the questions in the Stop and Savor section for Day One on page 17.
2. *Ask:* How do these words of Jesus—*What do you want?* and *Come and see.*—resonate in your life? (p. 19)
3. Call on a volunteer to read aloud John 2:4-12. Ask women to share any fresh insights they discovered from Jesus's miracle as well as any nudges toward obedience they identified on page 25.
4. Discuss answers to this question on page 30: *How do you think your life would be different if you had more personal time with the Lord each day?*
5. *Ask:* How did you summarize your personal takeaway to the big idea for Day 5: *Seek God-connection over self-protection.* (p. 37)?

REVIEW the Big Idea for each of the five days of study. Ask for final thoughts or questions regarding the study of God's plan this week.

PRAYER: To provide an opportunity for each woman to be prayed for during the week, lead each member of the group to write a prayer request on a provided note card, then pass that card to the woman on her right.

To access the video teaching sessions, use the instructions in the back of your Bible study book.

PEACE IN THE

POWER

OF JESUS

I TELL YOU THE TRUTH,

THOSE WHO LISTEN TO MY MESSAGE

AND BELIEVE IN GOD WHO SENT ME

HAVE ETERNAL LIFE. THEY WILL NEVER BE

CONDEMNED FOR THEIR SINS,

BUT THEY HAVE ALREADY PASSED

FROM DEATH INTO LIFE.

John 5:24

Day One
POWER TO KNOW

SCRIPTURE FOCUS

John 4:1-42

BIG IDEA

Peace is a Person.

"Pious Jews usually traveled around Samaria to avoid defilement, but for Jesus defilement came from within, not from without, and thus he took the shortest route, which was along the top of the ridge that passed by Sychar and Jacob's well."[1]

When I wrote an in-depth study of the names of God several years ago, one of the names I focused on was *Yahweh Shalom*—the Lord is peace. I studied Scriptures about peace trying to put together a road map for laying hold of peace. It felt formulaic and wooden. A friend reviewed what I'd written and mentioned that peace isn't a process found in a book, He is a Person. This truth rocked my world at the time.

Peace isn't something we create or conjure. It's a gift we receive through close relationship with the Prince of Peace. We need to hold onto this important truth as we continue to savor peace in a chaotic world through John's Gospel. Today we travel to the village of Sychar in Samaria where Jesus first revealed Himself as the Messiah. He unveiled His identity to a woman who became perhaps the first gospel evangelist.

A JEWISH MAN

READ JOHN 4:1-9 and identify the two barriers that caused the woman to be surprised by Jesus's request for a drink.

Jesus's request crossed gender and racial lines. The text indicates that Jesus was sitting beside the well and didn't move when the woman arrived. This was not the usual practice. As scholar Kenneth Bailey states: "On seeing her, Jesus was expected to courteously withdraw to a distance of at least twenty feet, indicating that it was both safe and culturally appropriate to approach the well."[2] Not only did Jesus stay put, He also spoke to her. To help us wrap our minds around how outlandish this would have been at the time, Bailey adds this insight: "In village society, a strange man does not even make eye contact with a woman in a public place."[3]

Jesus's request for water was not only directed toward a woman, but a Samaritan woman. In doing so, Jesus ignored more than five hundred years of hostility between Jews and Samaritans. When Assyria conquered the Northern Kingdom of Israel in 722 BC, they transported most of the Jews back to Assyria. They then repopulated the area with pagan people, who intermarried with the remaining Jews. This created a mixed-race people who pure-blood Jews viewed as ethnically and religiously corrupted. Thus the animosity. But Jesus set this acrimony aside and asked for a drink.

Jesus approached this Samaritan woman from a place of need. He elevated her worth by looking at her, speaking to her, and asking something from her.

> **What can you savor about Jesus from His encounter with the woman of Samaria?**

Village women in Jesus's day usually went to a well early in the morning or just before sundown to avoid the heat of the day. They traveled in groups for propriety's sake and to help each other lift the heavy jars.[4]

A RABBI

READ JOHN 4:10-18 and note what Jesus revealed about Himself in these verses.

Perhaps you wrote "gift from God" or "living water" or noted Jesus's ability to know the woman's marital history. But this nameless woman was thinking in terms of physical, tangible realities. She questioned His lack of bucket and rope. She wanted His water if it made her life easier. She was thinking only of temporal gifts from God.

She was focused on water to sustain physical life, while Jesus was pointing her to living water to provide eternal life. Jesus is the *Logos*— the Living Word who offers living water to us.

> **What can you savor about Jesus from this portion of His conversation with the woman of Samaria?**

A PROPHET

READ JOHN 4:19-24 and briefly explain the new issue the woman brought to Jesus now that she saw Him as a prophet.

The Samaritan woman's history had been exposed, but she didn't want to discuss those details. She wanted to talk about the correct place of worship. Jesus took the opportunity to clarify true worship.

What did He reveal in John 4:24?

Jesus wanted her to understand that God can't be confined to one location or defined in terms of a material being. Worship of Him isn't limited to a place or race. His character is infinitely beyond our limited views but intimately more personal than we could ever imagine.

The Samaritan woman focused on worship logistics, while Jesus brought it back to the heart.

How do we lose sight of what true worship of God is about?

THE MESSIAH

READ JOHN 4:25-42 and answer the following questions:

What did Jesus reveal to the woman in verse 26?

How did the woman respond to Jesus revealing Himself as Messiah?

What ultimately resulted from Jesus's conversation with the woman at the well (vv. 39-42)?

The woman experienced the spring of living water that Jesus referenced. She told everyone, "Come and see a man who told me everything I ever did!" (v. 29a). This was a sensational but effective advertisement because the people in the village knew her history. The text informs us that when she ran back to the village, she left her water bucket behind. She had come seeking well water but left carrying the promise of divine water.

Today's account reminds us that Jesus came to be our peace. He knows us fully—all our messy history—yet still came to earth to die for our sins. We might look for momentary peace from Amazon®, social media, a relationship, a new job, or a different church, but ultimately, peace is a Person, and His name is Jesus.

STOP AND SAVOR

Today we focused on this truth: *Peace is a Person.*

Summarize your personal takeaway from today's lesson.

What of Jesus's words and actions in this story stick out to you? Why?

How comforting and encouraging is it to know peace is not just a concept but a Person?

PRAYER

Lord, You are the Prince of Peace. Thank You for revealing Yourself to a Samaritan woman to help me know who You are. You are the Messiah! Help me not to get sidetracked by secondary issues that cause me to miss the rich truth of who You are. Help me to see and savor You today in my mind and in my heart. In Jesus's name, Amen.

Day Two
POWER TO HEAL

I spent way too many years attempting to conform my husband into a studious planner like me. Though attracted to Sean's spontaneity and wonder, I often tried to change him to be more serious and practical. As I began to recognize my tendencies, I was able to appreciate Sean for the unique way God made him and see how he is a good balance for me. Becoming self-aware helped me realize my wiring caused me to view Sean through a lens of unfair expectations. Just as our filters affect the way we see other people, they can also impact our understanding of God.

BIG IDEA

Identifying how our backstories impact our beliefs allows us to savor Jesus more authentically.

REQUIRING REACTION

READ JOHN 4:43-54 and answer the following questions:

What event does John remind us of that had previously happened in Cana? Why do you think this information is included in the text?

Who approached Jesus and what was his request?

Capernaum to Cana was about twenty-five miles via a road that climbs approximately 1,350 feet.[5] Being willing to make such a difficult journey helps us understand the desperation that prompted the man to beg Jesus to come.

How did Jesus respond?

What was the conclusion of this encounter?

The official underestimated Jesus's power. Jesus didn't need to be present to heal. Ultimately, the man believed without a sign. He accepted the word of the Word, starting with a crisis belief that later became a confirmed belief when he heard the timing of his son's recovery. This faith became contagious as his whole household ended up believing in Jesus.

Many Galileans craved amazement, while Jesus called them to dedication. They wanted a Savior who would heal them, lift them from poverty, and end their oppression. However, Jesus revealed Himself throughout this Gospel as much more than a circumstantial fix but as a Savior to be trusted with the outcomes in our lives.

What divine intervention are you asking God for today?

What could a next step of faith look like as you trust God with His answer?

To savor peace in this chaotic world where children get sick and disappointments abound, we need Scripture to shape our understanding of Jesus, His purposes, and His ways. We can ask God for anything in prayer, but we cannot limit Him to our parameters.

RELIGIOUS SUPERSTITION

READ JOHN 5:1-9a and either draw or briefly describe the scene below.

The lame man Jesus encountered at the pool had bought into a superstition about the waters' healing powers. Evidently something (perhaps a spring) caused the waters to periodically stir. When the disturbance occurred, people believed the first person in the water would be healed. The lame man's belief was rooted in mysticism, which seems incongruent with Judaism. Yet it was common for people "to believe in magic alongside institutional religion."[6]

What two inhibitors to healing did the lame man mention in verse 7?

He bemoaned his lack of help and others being faster than him getting into the waters. He hitched his healing hopes to a pool of water when the Giver of living water stood before him. He missed the significance of the question about true wellness because he could only process within the framework of his own categories and capabilities. Jesus didn't rebuke his limited understanding but instead expanded it with three commands.

What did Jesus tell the man to do in verse 8?

What needs healing in your life? It could be a relationship, finances, physical body, mind, spiritual health, or something else.

What excuses for not experiencing healing come to mind as you consider becoming whole in this area?

What might it look like to savor Jesus and His healing work in your life today?

Healing is a difficult topic. The poolside portico was filled with lame, paralyzed, and sick people, but Jesus approached only one man. Then, after the healing, Jesus "disappeared into the crowd" (John 5:13). (The Greek word used here means "to dodge."[7]) We don't know Jesus's motives regarding this biblical situation or His response to situations that happen in our lives. I've been asked questions like these:

- Why did God heal the cancer only to allow it to return?
- Why did their marriage heal while mine ended?
- Why did their grief subside while mine persists?

I'm sure you could add other difficult questions that don't have easy answers. Sometimes, the best we can do is acknowledge God's power to heal and accept His decisions regarding how and when it occurs. On the days it feels like we are ones who were dodged, may we find peace in God's sovereignty and presence.

RULES OVER RELATIONSHIP

READ JOHN 5:9b-16 and briefly explain what upset the Jewish leaders.

To learn a little more about the Pharisees, Sadducees, and Sanhedrin, check out the digging deeper article titled, "Jewish Leaders" found at **lifeway.com/ gospelofjohn.**

Jesus didn't heal on the Sabbath by accident. He knew the regulations about work on the Sabbath that had been added to the law. Perhaps He chose the day of rest to upset the religious leaders and bring the issue to the front. It's hard to wrap our minds around the religious leaders' focus on minutia in the midst of a miracle. Their lives revolved around the law. The law was good, but even good things can lead to spiritual blindness.

The government official was laser focused on his immediate need and limited God's power to a location. The lame man blended mysticism with his religious beliefs and limited God to a magical pool. The Jewish leaders elevated rules over relationships and limited when God's healing power could be expressed.

When John talked about "the Jews" or "the Jewish leaders" he was not making a racial or ethnic designation. He used that phrase to describe Jesus's religious opponents.[8]

Let's examine how your own backstory impacts your beliefs. Pick one of the following questions to answer and write a few notes about it: (1) What limits have you projected on God based on your personality? (2) How have your childhood/teen years contributed to the way you see God? (3) What role does media and culture have in the way you view Jesus?

John revealed Jesus unfiltered—the Son of God who was full of grace and truth. We want to savor Him through a biblical lens rather than through the filter of our culture and biases.

STOP AND SAVOR

Today we focused on this truth: *Identifying how our backstories impact our beliefs allows us to savor Jesus more authentically.*

Summarize your personal takeaway from today's lesson.

What stood out to you about what Jesus said and did?

How can you savor the peace of Jesus even when His actions and timing don't fulfill your requests?

Day Three
THE SOURCE OF POWER

Our focus this week is on savoring peace in the power of Jesus. We've seen Jesus's power on display in His interaction with the Samaritan woman and in healing the government official's son and the paralyzed man by the pool in Bethesda. Yet He faced opposition from Jewish leaders for displaying that power on the Sabbath.

When the leaders challenged Jesus, He responded by explaining His identity in relation to the Father. Jesus revealed Himself as the Son of God sent by God—and God Himself.

BIG IDEA
We can savor peace by finding our power and identity in the Son of God.

HIS IDENTITY

READ JOHN 5:16-23 and record what you learn about the Father and the Son in the chart below:

FATHER	SON
Verse 17	Verse 17
Verse 20	Verse 19
Verse 21	Verse 21
Verse 22	Verse 22

What stands out to you about the Father/Son relationship described by Jesus in these verses?

Based on these descriptions of the Father and the Son, how should people respond (v. 23)?

This passage shows the unity between the Father and the Son. They are both always working. And as the Father gives life, Jesus is entrusted with the authority to both give life and to judge. While the Son was not sent to condemn the world (John 3:17), He has the authority to judge those who choose unbelief.

Jesus knew His source of power and identity was in the Father. We find our identity in the Son and live by the power of His Holy Spirit. When we face criticism, knowing whose we are provides peace worth savoring. This passage not only teaches important Christology (the study of Christ) but also provides a model for us in times of opposition.

OUR IDENTITY

Write John 5:24 (our memory verse this week) below.

According to John 5:24, what do you know for sure about yourself today?

Here we find rich truth that can give us confidence. By faith in God through Christ we have passed from death to life and are no longer condemned. We are forever secure in Him. So when we face opposition or feel attacked—at work, in a relationship, or online—let's remember whose we are. Better yet, when our spiritual enemy accuses us, we don't have to listen to him. We stand in the truth of who we are in Christ. We're still going to make mistakes, mess up relationships and apologize, seek counsel in decisions, and need to change our behavior. But we always have hope in Him. Jesus said He could do nothing on His own, and neither can we. Instead, we rely on His power and who He says we are to shape our identity and confidence.

ALREADY AND NOT YET

READ JOHN 5:25-30 and record references to timing of important events in these verses:

Verse 25

Verses 28-29

Eschatology is "a branch of theology concerned with the final events in the history of the world or of humankind."[9]

Jesus said there is a time coming and is here now when the dead will hear His voice and those who listen will receive life (v. 25). This speaks to the ministry of Jesus, then and now, as the life-giver. There is present opportunity for salvation. However, there's a future time coming when all the dead will be raised, some to eternal life, some to judgment. This concept of already and not yet regarding God's kingdom can be difficult to wrap our minds around. However, Jesus used a phrase to describe Himself that would have helped the original audience to understand His meaning. It came from a prophecy in Daniel 7:13-14.

READ THAT PASSAGE below and underline the same phrases as found in John 5:27:

As my vision continued that night, I saw someone like a son of man coming with the clouds of heaven. He approached the Ancient One and was led into his presence. He was given authority, honor, and sovereignty over all the nations of the world, so that people of every race and nation and language would obey him. His rule is eternal—it will never end. His kingdom will never be destroyed.

DANIEL 7:13-14

With His use of "Son of Man," the Jews would likely have made the connection to Daniel's writing immediately and realized that Jesus was claiming to be both the Messiah and the Judge.[10] Passages like this one also give us reason to trust our Father with future events. The apostle Paul reminded us that right now we see only in part but one day God will make everything clear (1 Cor. 13:12). For now we accept that Christ has already come, and He has not yet returned.

WITNESSES

READ JOHN 5:31-47. **In this passage Jesus identified four witnesses who substantiated His claim. Draw a line to match the reference with the witness.**

vv. 32-35	Jesus's teaching and miracles
v. 36	The Father
vv. 37-38	The Scriptures
v. 39	John the Baptist

Witness is used forty-seven times in John's Gospel.[11]

When people got Jesus wrong, they got God wrong. Though the religious leaders knew the words of God, they did not know the Word of God (John 1:1,11), thus they did not know God Himself. As we think about what we look to for our own power and identity, we need a moment of self-reflection. Are we trusting in our knowledge, education, position, or experience more than Christ? Pastor Warren Wiersbe put it this way, "Does our knowledge of the Bible give us a 'big head' or a 'burning heart'?"[12] I'm not in any way discouraging us from reading and studying Scripture, for when we do so rightly, it always leads us to Jesus—to know Him better and become more like Him. It's just that we must do so with the right intention of the heart.

Jesus clearly showed Himself to be the Son of God who gives life and renders judgment but does nothing by Himself. The religious leaders of His day missed this truth. Let's make sure this doesn't happen to us.

STOP AND SAVOR

Today we focused on this truth: *We can savor peace by finding our power and identity in the Son of God.*

Summarize your personal takeaway from today's lesson.

What stood out to you about what Jesus said?

What attitude adjustments or action steps might the Holy Spirit be leading you to take in light of your study?

Day Four
MIRACULOUS POWER

SCRIPTURE FOCUS
John 6:1-21

BIG IDEA
We can savor peace by embracing Jesus for who He revealed Himself to be rather than who we want Him to be.

At a conference I attended, one of the speakers showed a series of images of Jesus commonly found on church walls. The first was smiling, playful Jesus—one with Him having fun with the children. Next the speaker showed good buddy Jesus—cool, friendly Jesus from an animated series. The third image was spooky Jesus—an expressionless face with a weird light glowing above Him. Finally, for humor, he showed a picture he referred to as bearded lady Jesus—a feminine looking face with a beard. His point was that each artist rendered Jesus from a personal point of view.

If you've seen drawings of Jesus, describe the background/ setting and what He looked like in those pictures.

Today, in John 6, we are going to find two stories of Jesus's miraculous power: the feeding of the multitudes and Jesus walking on water. The first is the only miracle (except for the resurrection) recorded in all four Gospels, and the second is recorded in every Gospel except Luke's. Our takeaway from these incredible displays will not be about sharing our food, the need to clean up leftovers, or remembering to bring extra life jackets on boat rides. Instead, we will see how these events clarify our theology regarding Jesus. In order to accomplish this, we will continually ask this question: Who is Jesus? We will lay aside mental pictures from the past and ask the Lord to reveal Himself anew to us through His Word.

The feeding of the multitudes
- Matthew 14:13-21
- Mark 6:31-44
- Luke 9:12-17
- John 6:1-14

Jesus walking on water
- Matthew 14:22-34
- Mark 6:45-53
- John 6:15-21

Normally, we pray at the end of each day's study, but before you open the text today, pray something like this:

Jesus, I want to know You. I long to experience Your power. Please check my motives that I might desire just You—not what You can do to fix my current problems or so that I can feel better about myself. Help me to see You clearly so I can love You with my whole heart. Use Your Word to shape my view of You—the Living Word. In Jesus's name, Amen.

THE NOTICER

READ JOHN 6:1-5 and answer the following questions:

Why was the crowd following Jesus?

What holy day did this event precede?

What question did Jesus ask Philip and why did He ask it?

Verse 5 says Jesus "saw a huge crowd of people," which seems like an insignificant detail. However, the Greek expression used here literally says Jesus "lifted up His eyes." It gives us an answer to our question, *Who is Jesus?* He noticed the people and had compassion for their physical needs. Jesus is the Son of God who lifts His eyes to notice what is happening in our world.

Jesus is God, and yet He notices you. As Jesus lifts His eyes in your direction today, what does He notice about your needs?

Philip, being from nearby Bethsaida, likely knew best how to obtain food in that area (John 1:44).[13]

THE TEACHER

READ JOHN 6:6-9. List the two disciples involved and a summary of their thoughts on the problem of hungry people:

VERSE(S)	DISCIPLE	SUMMARY
Verse 7		
Verses 8-9		

When Jesus asked Philip the question about a place to buy food, we can almost hear Philip doing mental arithmetic. He considered the amount of people to feed, then calculated the time and work needed to get that kind of money, and came up empty. However, he left Jesus completely out of his equations.

As did Andrew. He reported on the presence of a boy's lunch but knew the scarce amount would not be enough.

Jesus was testing His disciples to teach them. Where might He be doing this in your life? Here are some questions to consider:

Where have you been doing mental arithmetic? (If I do this, then it will fix that, etc.)

Where have you been focused on the enormity of the problem?

Where have you been looking with a scarcity mindset?

Jesus wants to teach us to think bigger. With Him, nothing is impossible. Even the big problems become an opportunity to get closer to Him.

In relation to the questions above, what has Jesus been teaching you lately?

THE GENEROUS HOST

READ JOHN 6:10-11 and number Jesus's actions in the order they appear in the verses from 1 to 5:

_____ He took the loaves.

_____ He distributed the fish.

_____ He gave thanks to God.

_____ He distributed the bread.

_____ He told everyone to sit down.

The five thousand represents men, so the actual number of people, including women and children, could have been significantly more than ten thousand.[14]

Jesus supernaturally provided. Although the crowd came for healing, Jesus was a generous host who fed them.

Reading accounts like this one realigns my thinking. So often I live with a scarcity mentality—as if God is limited.

Are there circumstances in your life where your thinking needs to expand regarding God's power to intervene? Explain.

THE GATHERER

READ JOHN 6:12-13. Why did Jesus say to gather up the leftovers?

John added details to the feeding of the multitudes account that were different than the other Gospels, including the proximity to Passover, the bread as barley loaves, and the reason for gathering remnants.

Jesus said nothing was to be wasted. He won't waste anything in your life either—your pain, your leftover fragments of a broken relationship, your consequences from poor choices. He will use it for your good and His glory.

THE PROPHET AND KING

READ JOHN 6:14-15 and answer the following questions:

Who did the people decide Jesus was?

What did they want to do about it?

What did Jesus do in response?

Jesus was a Prophet and King, but not in the sense the people wanted Him to be. They tried to force Him into their portrait of a warrior king with an earthly kingdom who would release them from political oppression. They couldn't reconcile how they wanted Him to act with how He acted. But Jesus the Prophet came as a Suffering Servant—to do God's will, not the people's will.

How have you seen people (media, people in your sphere) twist their understanding of Jesus to fit their mold?

It's well documented that the Sea of Galilee is prone to sudden storms. That's what likely occurred in the John 6 story of Jesus walking on the water.[15]

THE WATER WALKER

READ JOHN 6:16-21. What did Jesus call out to the men in the boat (v. 20)?

This story provides an interlude before Jesus connects the feeding of the crowd with His identity as the Bread of Life. It puzzles me that the disciples witnessed an incredible miracle, then only hours later a storm scared them. Yet, isn't that us? We see God work and our trust grows. But then the next storm frightens us. Jesus provides for us and calms our storms. He is the Creator who is in control of His creation. He is present with you.

Where is He calling you to release fear and savor His peace today? Reflect and journal some notes below.

We don't want to create an inaccurate picture of Jesus shaped by our feelings, personality, or what culture says about Him. We don't need a spooky Jesus or a buddy Jesus, we need the real Jesus.

STOP AND SAVOR

Today we focused on this truth: *We can savor peace by embracing Jesus for who He revealed Himself to be rather than who we want Him to be.*

Summarize your personal takeaway from today's lesson.

What stood out to you from Jesus's questions and statements?

How can you lift up your eyes (from screens, tasks, distractions) and see Jesus more clearly today?

Day Five

EXCHANGED POWER

SCRIPTURE FOCUS

John 6:22-71

BIG IDEA

When we focus on fulfilling our physical appetites, we can miss the One who longs to satisfy our spiritual hunger.

My best friend got a new puppy named Gemma. Gemma struggles with a misplaced appetite. She eats everything, including things that make her sick, like socks, balloons, and Wiffle® balls. While we chuckle at Gemma's strange obsession, sometimes it's not funny. Her stomach has been scanned more than once, and she has often lacked basic nutrition. She loves to eat but fills herself with objects that can't nourish her.

While we're not likely to eat socks, we also struggle with our appetites.

What's a food you've been craving lately?

I'm guessing most of us didn't write "salad" as our answers. We often desire food that brings instant pleasure but lacks needed nutrients. The food issues for Jesus's original audience looked a little different than ours. Most of them weren't trying to limit their food intake but rather working to ensure they had enough to survive.

Jesus had provided bread and fish for a huge crowd who now wanted more of that kind of miracle. But Jesus didn't come just to fill their stomachs. He cared for physical needs but longed for them to prioritize their spiritual hunger. Like this crowd, we can overfocus on the urgent and miss the important.

SPENDING YOUR ENERGY

READ JOHN 6:22-29 and answer the following questions:

Why did Jesus say the people were seeking Him?

What did Jesus say the people should work for or spend their energy doing?

What was their request, and how did Jesus reply in verses 28-29? What did Jesus mean?

The people couldn't lift their minds above the physical necessities of life. Jesus was not commanding them to stop working for a living; He was urging them to focus their main quest on food that doesn't perish. We can also become captives to our physical longings. Much of our lives revolve around food.

What are some ways you have spent time and energy on food and mealtimes the last few days?

Maybe you went to the grocery store, drove through a fast-food line, or made plans to meet a friend for lunch. We can't help but spend some energy on feeding ourselves. Jesus isn't shaming anyone for needing food, but He knows the weakness that accompanies spiritual emptiness.

What are some ways we can feed our spiritual appetite?

The restlessness of our souls won't be satiated with media, hobbies, or human relationships. Instead, we must spend our energy on eternal pursuits such as prayer, God's Word, rest, godly community, and other spiritual practices that help us feast on the Bread of Life.

SEEING BEYOND

READ JOHN 6:30-59 and look for repeated words and phrases. Write the ones that stand out to you below.

The phrase "I tell you the truth" or "truly, truly I say unto you" (John 6:32,47,53) is the Greek word for "amen" repeated twice. Jesus used it for emphasis at the beginning of important revelations.

I'm guessing "bread" was probably one of the words you identified.

What smells, tastes, or images come to mind as you think about bread?

My husband makes bread in our electric bread maker. I can barely wait for it to cool before slathering it with butter or honey! It is definitely something to savor. In this passage, Jesus revealed Himself to be the source of spiritual nourishment. The crowd just wanted what Jesus could give them, not Jesus Himself. They asked for more signs and referenced the manna God gave the Israelites as a temporary provision during their wilderness years (Ex. 16:14-15). They likely mentioned manna because of "a Jewish expectation that, when the Messiah came, He would renew the miracle of manna."[16] They wanted more evidence and more bread. We can relate to the desire for more.

Our Amazon packages keep coming because we want more stuff. A promotion at work leads us to climb even higher in search of more recognition. This message hits close to home as I realize how consumed I can be about things that won't last forever.

For example, I've been fretting over light fixtures we are replacing and picking our health insurance plan for next year. These tasks certainly aren't sinful, they just shouldn't fill all the space in my mind and heart so that I forget what matters most. We often aren't doing the things of God because our lives are overloaded with everything else. Jesus calls us to see beyond the earthly to the eternal and prioritize things that will last.

Take a moment to list what has been occupying your mental and emotional real estate this past week.

"I am the bread of life" (John 6:35) is the first of the seven "I AM" statements Jesus made in the Gospel of John.

Eating the Bread of Life means engaging in a real relationship with the Living God. The people in John 6 wanted physical power to fix their earthly problems, but Jesus offered spiritual power to savor His peace for all eternity.

STAYING THE COURSE

READ JOHN 6:60-71 and identify the responses of the following people:

Many of His disciples (v. 66)

Simon Peter (v. 68)

Jesus's true disciples stayed the course through miraculous signs and hard spiritual truths. Those who were superficially attracted to the sensational fell away. Superficial belief falters, but steadfast faith remains. We don't move to steadfast faith by trying harder because Jesus said that human effort accomplishes nothing. Instead, we need to eat the Bread of Life. We realize and proclaim as Peter did, that our only hope is in Jesus. Only He has the words of life. So we trust Him, surrender, and follow.

STOP AND SAVOR

Today we focused on this truth: *When we focus only on fulfilling our physical appetites, we can miss the One who longs to satisfy our spiritual hunger.*

Summarize your personal takeaway from today's lesson.

What surprised you about Jesus's responses or questions?

How does what you read and studied today help you savor the peace of Jesus?

The term "disciples" used in verse 66 is a blanket term referring to people who were following Jesus to learn from His messages. The Greek word for "disciple" simply means "learner."[17]

PRAYER

Jesus, help me to savor my relationship with You. I don't want to treat You like a vending machine—just looking for what I can get from Your power. Instead, help me to spend my energy on eternal things, see beyond temporary circumstances, and stay the course in my relationship with You. Help me to savor peace in Your power even when I can't see or feel it. I believe You are the Bread of Life! In Jesus's name, Amen.

Video Viewer Guide

Signs point to something _____.

The power we need is not a circumstantial _____ but a change of _____.

1. _____ and _____ are postures of power (John 4:43-50).

2. _____ lameness is more crippling than _____ lameness (John 5:6-9,14).

3. Our physical _____ can absorb our attention away from spiritual _____ (John 6:14-15;26-30;35).

Jesus is the _____ of life.

CHALLENGE FOR THE WEEK: Plan a spiritual meal and a spiritual snack.

(Answers are available on p. 185.)

GROUP DISCUSSION GUIDE

SHARE: What is one of your favorite carbohydrates to eat? (Think: bread, potatoes, cake, etc.)

WATCH the video "Session Three: Savoring Peace in the Power of Jesus" together and follow along with the viewer guide on the previous page.

MEMORY VERSE: Review John 5:24 and provide time for group members to recite it aloud.

VIDEO DISCUSSION

1. *Ask:* What reason for not praying mentioned in the video do you best identify with? What has helped increase your consistency and tenacity in prayer?

2. *Discuss:* Which of the following three statements connected to the three signs covered in the video resonated most in your life and why?
   - *Asking and believing are postures of power.*
   - *Spiritual lameness is more crippling than physical lameness.*
   - *Our physical appetites can absorb our attention away from spiritual nourishment.*

STUDY DISCUSSION

1. Encourage participants to share responses from their answers to the questions in the Stop and Savor section for Day One on page 45.

2. Call on a volunteer to read aloud John 4:43-54. Discuss participants' answers to these two questions on page 47: *What divine intervention are you asking God for today? What could a next step of faith look like as you trust God with His answer?*

3. *Ask:* How have the truths found in this week's memory verse (John 5:24) shaped your identity? How can this Scripture be used to combat shame or discouragement?

4. Discuss what stood out to you about Jesus's feeding of the five thousand (John 6:1-15). (You can use the prompts of Noticer, Teacher, Generous Host, Gatherer, Prophet, and King.)

5. *Ask:* What are some ways we can feed our spiritual appetite? (p. 63) Brainstorm together any additional ideas that can be applied this week.

REVIEW the Big Idea for each of the five days of study. Ask for final thoughts or questions regarding the study of God's power this week.

PRAYER: Share prayer requests and lead your group to record them on the tops of the starting pages for each day of study for the coming week (Session Four). When they open their books each day, this will prompt them to begin that day of study by praying for the needs of others in their group.

To access the video teaching sessions, use the instructions in the back of your Bible study book.

PEACE IN THE

PATIENCE

OF JESUS

LOOK BENEATH THE SURFACE

SO YOU CAN JUDGE CORRECTLY.

John 7:24

Day One

PATIENT WITH PEOPLE

SCRIPTURE FOCUS
John 7:1-36

BIG IDEA
People may try to rush us, but we can savor peace in God's timing.

When I served on the Parent Teacher Organization (PTO) during my children's elementary years, I disliked the monthly meetings. We spent a lot of time discussing fundraisers, classroom parties, and listening to varied opinions. I struggle with meetings in general because I struggle with patience. Once I've decided in my own head how things should be done, I'm easily annoyed by critics, questions, or bunny trails. Writing this down is very convicting.

Can you relate? Do you need patience for those who have different opinions, take longer to express their thoughts, have a lot of questions, or criticize without having all the facts?

What current situations in your life present an opportunity for patience?

John's Gospel places Jesus in attendance at several of the Jewish celebrations. To learn more about these holy days, check out the digging deeper article titled, "The Festivals" found online at **lifeway. com/gospelofjohn.**

Today we will discover Jesus's patience with His family, His critics, and the crowd. Each of these groups attempted to direct Jesus regarding where He went, when He went, and what He should say and do. Jesus was patient with them, and He is also patient with us. People may try to rush us, but we can savor peace in God's timing.

PATIENT WITH FAMILY

READ JOHN 7:1-9 and answer the following questions:

What Festival was being celebrated?

Why did Jesus's brothers urge Him to go to Judea?

What do you think was their motivation?

What was Jesus's response to His brother's mocking statements? What did He mean?

In Jesus's day, if the powers that be in Judea were looking for you, it would be safer for you to stay in Galilee, and vice versa, since the two regions were under separate jurisdictions.[1]

Rather than approach Jesus's miracles and messages with belief, or just curiosity, Jesus's brothers acted as self-appointed campaign managers goading Him to do His works in public with the Feast of Tabernacles being a prime-time opportunity. But they were ignorant of His purpose and didn't have His best interest at heart. Jesus wouldn't be rushed. He listened to the Father for instruction. He wasn't going to let His brothers pressure Him into proving Himself. His time had not yet come.

Jesus didn't deceive them by saying He wasn't going, then going later. Their timing and what they wanted Him to do was different than His timing and purpose. He would eventually go, but He could not celebrate as a normal participant at the Feast of Tabernacles because He was the fulfillment of it. John 1:14 revealed that Jesus "dwelt among us" (CSB). "Dwelt" is the Greek word *skenoo*, which means "to fix one's tabernacle."[2] Ironically, while the Jews were busy setting up their tabernacles, they didn't realize that the fulfillment of their ceremonies walked among them.[3]

While His brothers used rhetoric to provoke Him, Jesus didn't argue or rebuke them. He tried to explain in a way their limited understanding could bear. He knew they would eventually have their eyes opened to the truth and be counted among the church's leaders (Acts 1:14; 1 Cor. 9:5; Gal 1:19). But, at this point, Jesus simply said, "My time has not yet come" (John 7:8).

John's emphasis on pace and timing in the ministry of Jesus is unique from the Synoptic Gospels of Matthew, Mark, and Luke.

Patience with family can be challenging. Jesus exercised patience toward His earthly brothers when they taunted Him. With His power we can show patience toward our family members as well.

How do you need to show patience toward a close friend or family member this week? Fill in the square next to the actions you will take, or add your own. You can choose more than one.

☐ Listen without interrupting in your next conversation.
☐ Slow down to someone's pace (speed of walking, talking).
☐ Write down what you want to communicate in your journal before saying it.
☐ Pray daily throughout this week for the person with whom you feel impatient.
☐ Identify what rouses your impatience and surrender it.
☐ _____
☐ _____

It takes time to develop and maintain patience in our relationships, especially with close family. Be persistent, and recognize that both you and your family members can benefit from practicing patience together.

PATIENT WITH THE CROWD

READ JOHN 7:10-24 and write verse 24 in your own words below.

The New Living Translation says, "Look beneath the surface so you can judge correctly." This was the heart of Jesus's message as He patiently attempted to help the crowd understand His identity.

The crowd was divided on whether Jesus was a good man or a fraud. When He stepped up to teach, the people were amazed at His teaching. But to the Pharisees in the crowd, He was a threat to their authority and traditions. They criticized Him for healing on the Sabbath, so Jesus patiently introduced Moses into the conversation to help them recognize their own standards of precedence. When two instructions collided, the greater command took precedence. Jesus used circumcision and the Sabbath as His examples.

Our lens for seeing Jesus as He really is can become clouded with the traditions in which we were raised, media messages regarding God, or our own misconceptions about Him. Yet, Jesus patiently calls us to see beneath the surface so that we can judge correctly.

Think about a current frustrating or challenging situation regarding people (anything from a small annoyance to a severed relationship).

What are the surface details of what happened?

What might the Lord want you to see beneath the surface as you consider the feelings involved, past history, and potential growth in the situation?

Let's dig deep so we don't miss the eternal work God wants to do in our lives.

PATIENT WITH CRITICS

READ JOHN 7:25-36 and summarize the reasons the following people groups rejected Jesus:

The local people of Jerusalem (v. 27)

Pharisees (vv. 31-32)

How did these two groups fail to look beneath the surface so they could judge correctly?

The stumbling block for the people of Jerusalem was bad theology. They assumed the Messiah would instantaneously appear rather than be born into a family. The Pharisees felt threatened by His popularity. I can't help but be amazed at Jesus's patience with both groups.

In verse 30 we find John repeating the phrase, "because his time had not yet come." God's sovereign plan unfolded according to His timetable. Jesus didn't allow people to rush Him—whether they were family, crowds, or critics. He followed God's plan one step at a time.

STOP AND SAVOR

Today we focused on this truth: *People may try to rush us, but we can savor peace in God's timing.*

Summarize your personal takeaway from today's lesson.

How was Jesus's patience displayed in today's passage?

What did Jesus say about Himself that you can savor today?

Day Two

A PATIENT INVITATION

Our family took a trip out west with friends and extended family several years ago. We saw incredible sights, including a beautiful waterfall at Yellowstone National Park. However, to get to this waterfall, we had to hike a few miles on a hot day in July. My husband, Sean, was carrying a small cooler containing water bottles for our immediate family. He wanted to linger at the Grand Prismatic Spring (a colorful hot spring) longer than the rest of the antsy group so he decided to meet us later on the trail. Unfortunately, Sean thought he spotted us going a different direction so we never met up. By the time we returned to the car, we were mildly dehydrated and out of sorts.

When was the last time you remember being thirsty and not having access to water?

In today's text, we'll find Jesus looking beneath the surface of physical thirst to address our spiritual dryness. He invites us to drink His living water.

DYING OF THIRST

READ JOHN 7:37-38 and answer these questions:

On which day of the Festival of Tabernacles did this occur?

Summarize Jesus's invitation, including who could respond and what they would receive.

SCRIPTURE FOCUS
John 7:37-52

BIG IDEA
We are all dying of spiritual thirst, and Jesus invites us to drink His living water.

What did Jesus mean by "living water" (v. 38)?

Part of the week-long Feast of Tabernacles (Booths/Shelters) was a water ceremony in which the people followed a priest who carried water in a golden cup from the pool of Siloam to the temple. This was to remind the Jews of God's miraculous provision of water from the rock while their ancestors were in the wilderness.[4] This procession was repeated once each day and seven times on the last day of the celebration.

More than once God miraculously provided water for the Israelites wandering in the desert. God turned bitter water into drinking water (Ex. 15:22-27). Moses struck a rock and water poured out (Ex. 17:1-7). In the wilderness, water was a life-or-death situation.[5]

In today's passage, Jesus didn't issue a collective call to a water ritual, but invited His hearers to an individual response of faith that would result in "rivers of living water" (John 7:38), flowing from the believer's heart to provide perpetual satisfaction of spiritual thirst.

How have you experienced spiritual thirst, and how has Jesus quenched your thirst as the Living Water?

The people were sincere in their celebration of the Festival of Tabernacles, but they were missing the One who fulfilled its meaning. Jesus didn't mandate their belief but rather invited them to consider His invitation. The Lord continues patiently inviting today rather than forcing Himself upon His creation.

THE PROMISE OF THE SPIRIT

READ JOHN'S EDITORIAL COMMENT IN JOHN 7:39 and record what you learn about the Holy Spirit.

John explained that the "rivers of living water" (v. 38) Jesus promised was the Holy Spirit. He would be given to everyone who believes, but not until after Jesus ascended, or "entered into his glory" (v. 39).

God's Spirit was involved in Creation and present among God's people during Old Testament times—empowering certain people for specific tasks. After Christ ascended to heaven, the Spirit came powerfully at Pentecost (Acts 2), permanently living within every person who followed Jesus from then on.

Pentecost marked the beginning of the apostles' public ministry and the spread of Christianity beyond its initial followers.

How have you experienced the Holy Spirit working in your life?

If you haven't sensed Him at work or would like to see His guidance in your life grow, how can you be more aware and connected to God's Spirit who lives within you?

In our study of John, our focus is savoring the peace of Jesus in a chaotic world. Read the verses below and circle the fruit found in the subtitle of our Bible study:

> But the Holy Spirit produces this kind of fruit in our lives: love, joy, peace, patience, kindness, goodness, faithfulness, gentleness, and self-control. There is no law against these things!
> **GALATIANS 5:22-23**

As we pursue the peace and patience of Jesus, we are reminded that we can't manufacture either on our own. We savor both through God's Spirit who lives in us.

DEBATING THE SOURCE

READ JOHN 7:40-53 and fill in the chart below with the different responses to Jesus's invitation:

VERSE(S)	PERSON/ PEOPLE	RESPONSE REGARDING JESUS
Verses 40-44	The crowd	
Verses 45-46	Temple guards	
Verses 47-49	Pharisees	
Verses 50-51	Nicodemus	
Verse 52	Pharisees (part 2)	

Some of the people thought Jesus might be the prophet whom Moses spoke about in Deuteronomy 18:15. There are other references to this "Prophet" in John 1:21,25; 6:14.

Some of the crowd believed Jesus was the Prophet, and some said He was the Messiah. Others had inaccurate information about Jesus's birthplace. The religious leaders scoffed about Him. Jesus didn't grade Himself based on the varied responses to His invitation. Instead, He listened to the Father for His timing and message.

How do you compare the way people responded to Jesus then to how they respond to Him today?

This passage reminds me that it's much easier to label people than listen to the facts. When the religious leaders couldn't answer the arguments of the temple guards or Nicodemus, they attacked the speaker. They even used racial prejudice against Galileans, which "was common in antiquity."[6]

Many religious people in the crowd at the Feast of Tabernacles missed the peace of God because of their preconceived ideas and superficial understandings. We want to learn from them what not to do so that we can savor the peace of Jesus and drink the living water of His Spirit today.

STOP AND SAVOR

Today we focused on this truth: *We are all dying of spiritual thirst, and Jesus invites us to drink His living water.*

Summarize your personal takeaway from today's lesson.

What stood out to you about what Jesus said?

What did you notice about His patience?

Day Three
A PATIENT RESPONSE

BIG IDEA
Jesus won't
condemn you,
so you can stop
condemning
yourself.

I'm sitting at my laptop debating which story of personal failure to tell you. I can recall many times when I said the wrong thing, took a course of action contrary to God's Word, or misread a situation. Because I'm a Bible study author, people sometimes assume I'm a better person than I am. However, I know all too well my bent toward selfishness, laziness, excess, and pride. This awareness of sin is vital when it comes to repentance but can be a danger when it leads me to self-condemnation. Perhaps you can relate to beating yourself up over your sin rather than repenting of it.

Are there condemning thoughts rolling around in your mind lately? If so, write a few of them below.

Negative self-talk leads us away from God. Rather than throw stones at ourselves for being sinful humans, we can savor peace in this truth: Jesus won't condemn you, so you can stop condemning yourself.

Before we dig into today's passage to see Jesus's radical response toward sin, we need to discuss a controversy that surrounds these verses.

Regarding John 8:1-11, you may see a note/footnote in your Bible that reads something like this: *The most ancient Greek manuscripts do not include John 7:53–8:11.* Without getting too deep into the weeds, let's dispel any confusion surrounding this notation. Translators of the Bible relied on a variety of early manuscripts to produce the Bible you are using today. Textual criticism is a science that evaluates thousands of surviving copies of the New Testament to determine credibility. The consensus of textual critics is that this account was not a part of the original Gospel of John but is probably an authentic story that is helpful for us to understand the purpose and work of Jesus.

A SETUP FOR A SAVIOR

READ JOHN 8:1-11 and write brief observations regarding these individuals/groups.

- Jesus

- The crowd

- Scribes (teachers of religious law) and Pharisees

- The woman caught in adultery

The technical term for John 8:1-11 is *agraph* which is "an unwritten story known to the church and passed on in oral form and finally recorded in some copies of the Gospel of John."[7]

I'm wondering why the man caught in adultery wasn't mentioned. The experts in the law certainly knew that both participants were required to be put to death (Lev. 20:10; Deut. 22:22). Another question that comes to mind is how the religious leaders happened to catch this couple in the act. Several scholars speculate that perhaps the scribes and Pharisees set up this scenario in order to trap Jesus in a no-win situation.

The religious leaders didn't ask a hypothetical question. They put the accused woman right in front of Jesus. She became a prop in their plan to force Him to either break Roman law or disagree with Moses. The Romans denied the Jews the right to put anyone to death (John 18:31). So if Jesus initiated a stoning, nearby Roman soldiers would likely rush to the commotion and arrest Jesus. If Jesus disagreed with stoning, then it would discredit Him as contradicting the Law of Moses. The religious leaders wanted Him gone by any means necessary. They cared more about turf than truth.

In Jesus's day, the temple area had large walkways throughout. At the north end, Herod the Great had built a military fort knowing that much civil unrest was connected with the temple. Roman officers patrolled the walkways looking for any signs of disturbance among the people, particularly during festivals.[8]

> **How did Jesus handle what appeared to be a no-win situation? (Consider specifically His pace, His posture, and His words.)**

Jesus was patient when cornered. He didn't use the tactics we saw employed in the previous chapter by the religious elite: attack the speaker (John 7:44-48), twist the truth (v. 49), and redirect with prejudice (v. 52).

Jesus took His time, physically got low, and spoke few but compelling words. Whether we are the one caught in sin, part of the crowd drifting away, or having a Pharisee moment of manipulation, Jesus responds to us with grace and truth.

R. C. Sproul states "This is the only mention in Scripture of Jesus writing anything."[9]

A PATIENT RESPONSE

There is much speculation about what Jesus wrote in the dirt. What interpretive guesses have you heard taught and what's your opinion?

Some say Jesus wrote a list of the accusing men's specific sins.[10] Others surmise it could have been any number of Old Testament verses about mercy.[11] A western mindset often leans toward the questions involving how and what, while an eastern mind contemplates why and who. So if it's not in the story, that gives us a clue that our focus should be elsewhere.

There's one thing to note before we move on: the text clarifies Jesus wrote with His finger. I think that's significant. The Ten Commandments were written by the finger of God (Ex. 31:18; Deut. 9:10). So the scribes and Pharisees were challenging the writer of the law. While Jesus's words in the dirt are not revealed, we do get a glimpse into His authority as the Author of the standards the religious leaders were attempting to use to trap Him.

Knowing Jesus has the authority to judge, how does His response to the woman reflect how Jesus deals with your sin?

Notice that Jesus's finger was not pointed in accusation at the woman. This confrontation started with the Law of Moses and ended with the law of Christ. Jesus shifted the hostility of the religious leaders from the woman to Himself, exchanging grace for disgrace. He offered up His life to pay the price of sin on the cross—for the woman caught in adultery and for us. We can savor peace as we view our sin in light of His finished work of atonement.

SIN NO MORE

Jesus was the One worthy to throw a stone, but He didn't. He didn't condemn the woman, but He also didn't overlook her self-destructive lifestyle. He instructed her to turn from sin because He knew its destructive power and its deathly penalty which He would take upon Himself. His grace and truth echoes into our own battles with sin. So let's transfer the energy we use beating ourselves up to cultivating a heart of repentance.

> **Turning from sin and turning to God needs to be a daily practice. Take time now to bring your sins before God and ask for His help in turning in a new direction. Feel free to journal your prayer below.**

STOP AND SAVOR

Today we focused on this truth: *Jesus won't condemn you, so you can stop condemning yourself.*

> **Summarize your personal takeaway from today's lesson.**

> **What do you want to savor about the character of Christ from today's passage and why?**

> **What words of grace and truth is God speaking to you currently?**

PRAYER

Jesus, I may not know what You wrote in the dirt that day, but I know You have the authority to judge. Thank You for not condemning me. Help me to think about the cross and the sacrifice You made for my sin more frequently. Jesus, Your kindness leads me to repentance. Today, I turn from my sin and turn to You. Reveal Your grace and truth to me. In Jesus's name, Amen.

Day Four

TRUE FREEDOM

BIG IDEA

True freedom includes the ability to say no to the short-term pleasures of sin and yes to long-term peace found only through Christ.

I recently discovered that more than four hundred types of phobias exist![12] Some sound strange, like fear of cheese or fear of developing a phobia. Others, like fear of heights or public speaking, don't surprise me. I did a quick personal inventory to determine if I have any phobias and realized my tendency toward claustrophobia. If a family member puts his or her arm or leg on me while we are watching a movie, I have to get it off so I can breathe. I know it's weird, but it's one of the areas where I crave freedom.

If you had to pick one area where you don't like having constraints, would it be free time, free speech, financial freedom, freedom of physical movement, or something else?

In our culture, freedom is often defined as the ability to do anything we want. Today we will discover that true freedom includes the ability to say no to the short-term pleasures of sin and yes to the long-term peace found only through Christ.

I write those words understanding the tension of how hard it is to overcome sin—especially the repetitive ones. It can feel like a game of Whac-A-Mole™. We experience freedom in one area only to find ourselves enslaved in another. As we get into the text, be gentle with yourself. Rather than concentrate on areas of past failure, focus on future freedom.

THE LIGHT OF THE WORLD

READ JOHN 8:12-20 and finish the sentence below in your own words:

Because Jesus is the Light of the world, those who follow Him _____

_____.

During the Festival of Tabernacles, four massive lamps in the temple's court of women provided light where a great celebration took place every evening.[13] This illumination served as a reminder for the people of the pillar of fire that led their ancestors in the wilderness.[14] Jesus used the illustration of light—a common metaphor in the Old Testament (Ps. 89:15; Prov. 13:9; Isa. 5:20; 51:4) to reveal that while the lamps would be extinguished after the festival, His light would continue forever.[15]

Life is a key word in John and points us back to the prologue (John 1:4-5).

This is the second of seven I AM statements recorded in John's Gospel. The first was Jesus's revelation as the Bread of Life. As the Light of the world, Jesus brings brightness but also exposure. Light reveals what sinners like to hide in the darkness.

As you evaluate your thoughts, your media choices, and your words, what does God's light of both conviction and hope expose and encourage in your life?

Which of your patterns and habits are bringing life and which are bringing death to your relationships, spiritual growth, and/or physical health?

Jesus came to bring us light and life—not just for a temporary event or experience—but forever. However, many in the crowd had questions about His bold claims.

DEPENDENT ON THE FATHER

READ JOHN 8:21-30 and describe in your own words the relationship between Jesus and the Father.

There is double meaning in Jesus's reference to being lifted up. He would be lifted up on the cross but also lifted up to the Father, returning to the glory He enjoyed with the Father before the incarnation.[16]

Jesus modeled what it meant to live in dependence on the Father. If He—fully man but also God incarnate—totally relied on the Father, how much more should we lean on Him in our neediness?

Identify at least one way you can pursue greater dependence on God in the days ahead.

If you had trouble answering the previous question, don't worry. The last part of chapter 8 reveals practical truths to shape our understanding of what it means to live reliant on God.

TRUTH THAT BRINGS FREEDOM

READ JOHN 8:31-59 and answer the following questions:

What did Jesus say is the mark of a true disciple (v. 31)?

Summarize what Jesus said about freedom in verses 32-36.

What do those who belong to God gladly do (v. 47)?

Verse 30 reveals that many believed in Him, but in the following verses, Jesus showed their faith to be superficial belief. The crowd believed Jesus as long as He didn't clash with their prejudices and religious bias. The Jews grasped for freedom in their ancestry to Abraham, but real freedom is found only in Christ, because as He said, He Himself is the God of Abraham (v. 58).

This reminds us again of our memory verse this week—to look beneath the surface so we can judge correctly.

Is there something you know the Bible says to do and you aren't doing it? Is there something the Bible says not to do and you know you are doing it? Explain.

Taking the time to evaluate our thoughts is important because truth gets muddy in our chaotic world. Culture attempts to reshape our worldview and ultimately our values. We struggle to live in the truth that brings freedom. When I first read this passage, I was discouraged by the disparity I confronted: Jesus's light, my darkness; His dependence on the Father, my independence; His call to truth, my clinging to lies that lead to bondage. I identified with the crowd, full of excuses and questions. Perhaps you relate.

The good news is that our struggles don't condemn us and we don't have to fix our failures on our own. Jesus reminds us we were created for connection with our Creator—a connection He established through His sacrifice. As we repent and obey, God continues to conform us to the image of His Son.

We won't find peace in defending our positions or arguing over nuances. Peace is found in the light. Today we can embrace afresh our neediness of Him and grow in the truth that brings freedom.

STOP AND SAVOR

Today we focused on this truth: *True freedom includes the ability to say no to the short-term pleasures of sin and yes to long-term peace found only through Christ.*

Summarize your personal takeaway from today's lesson.

As you observed Jesus's relationship with His Father, what resonated with you and why?

How are you inspired to walk in freedom today?

PRAYER

Lord, help me to embrace Your freedom. I don't want to live enslaved to sin when You paid such a high price to set me free. Guide me away from sin and toward You. I yield myself today, recognizing my need for daily dependence on You. In Jesus's name, Amen.

Day Five
PATIENT WITH SPIRITUAL BLINDNESS

SCRIPTURE FOCUS
John 9

BIG IDEA
When we recognize our spiritual blindness, Jesus can open our eyes to see our need for Him.

I'll never forget the drive home from getting my glasses when I was in fifth grade. I commented to my mom that I could see all the branches on the trees. Before I got glasses I viewed trees from a distance as blobs without detail. I thought everyone did. Only when I got corrective lenses did I realize what my eyes had failed to see. In our study of John 9 today, we'll discover we can have spiritual blind spots. When I say blind spots, I'm talking about things in our lives that block or hinder us from seeing the truth clearly. When we recognize these weaknesses, Jesus can open our eyes to see our need for Him.

READ JOHN 9:1-12 and either summarize the action in a few sentences or draw a picture of what took place in the boxes below.

VERSES 1-5	VERSES 6-7	VERSES 8-12

Making the mud would have been equated with the kneading of bread, which was forbidden on the Sabbath. Later the Talmud (commentary on Jewish Law) would specify the making of mud as a violation of Sabbath rest.[17]

What stands out to you about Jesus's words or actions from this account?

Throughout this chapter we find echoes to the prologue of John's Gospel. The creation references, including light and mud,[18] frame this story not as an interaction between doctor and patient but between Creator and created. God created man from the dust, and Jesus uses some of that dirt in a redemptive act of restoration. However, He had something much bigger in mind than just physically restoring sight to one man. One commentator summed it up this way: "True blindness goes much deeper than the eyes; it is a disease that creates blindness to oneself."[19]

We all struggle with spiritual blind spots—areas in our lives where we lack awareness of our skewed perspectives. The disciples displayed one in this story. They saw the man as an opportunity for a theological discussion rather than a person in need of compassion (John 9:2). Along with most people in antiquity, they sourced suffering, including blindness, with personal sin.[20] Jesus patiently explained the truth, then exemplified it. As we look at the response of the Pharisees, the man's parents, and the man himself—we'll discover that viewing a situation through the wrong lens can lead to blind spots. We can miss seeing a situation clearly when our perspective is skewed from looking through a lens of criticism, fear, insecurity, pride, selfishness, or some other negatively influencing filter.

THE LENS OF CRITICISM

READ JOHN 9:13-34. Who saw this situation through the lens of criticism and how did they express it (vv. 16,24,28-29,34)?

Jesus's friction with the Pharisees builds throughout John's Gospel. In chapter 5, they criticized Him for the similar offense of healing a lame man on the Sabbath. In chapter 8, they brought a woman caught in adultery trying to trap and discredit Him. In this chapter they threatened to ban anyone following Jesus from the synagogue. Seeing things through the lens of criticism caused them to miss the peace of God through His sent One.

We may not be opposing Jesus like the Pharisees, but we must still fight against a critical spirit. I personally struggle with the lens of criticism. I don't want to elevate rules over relationships or embrace a fault-finding posture, but I'm constantly fighting against these tendencies.

Is seeing things through the lens of criticism a struggle for you? If so, how? If nothing rises to the surface, write a prayer asking God to reveal any areas you might be missing.

Pastor and author Edward Klink said, "The statement that 'he is old enough' is an idiom which expresses that a person is of the legal age to speak on his own behalf."[21]

THE LENS OF FEAR

When questioned, what was the parents' response to the miracle and why did they respond this way (vv. 22-23)?

Being banned from the synagogue was rare in Jesus's day, but it was severe.[22] The synagogue was central to Jewish life. To be banned would carry consequences for a Jewish family's livelihood, social status, and religious community. These parents avoided answering the Pharisee's questions out of fear.

How does fear impact your witness and obedience to Christ?

Maybe you struggle to share the gospel with someone, to follow a prompting of the Holy Spirit, or tithe because of fear. I relate to these struggles. Instead of beating yourself up about it, bring your fears to the Lord.

Ask God to reveal where you might be wearing the lens of fear rather than faith. Lay those fears before Him and ask for help to walk in faith and boldness.

THE LENS OF FAITH

Summarize the healed man's second encounter with the Pharisees. Note his proclamation, explanation, and challenge to them (vv. 24-34).

The man didn't have all the answers. He didn't know whether Jesus was a prophet or if He was a sinner. But he knew that he had been blind and now he could see. He took what He did know to be true about Jesus and proclaimed it. His testimony reminds us we don't have to have all the answers to be a witness.

> **READ JOHN 9:35-41.** Explain what took place between Jesus and the healed man.

The healed man had received physical sight earlier, but he gained spiritual sight when he declared, "I believe, Lord" (v. 38). Jesus patiently declared that He is the light that allows each of us to see God clearly. We can either continue to struggle with blind spots or put on the lens of faith and ask God to open our eyes to Him at work all around us.

I didn't realize how skewed my physical vision was until I got glasses. In the same way, sin distorts our view of the world, our own righteousness, and God. While all of us may not need corrective lenses for physical vision, all of us need God glasses to illuminate our path spiritually. True sight is contingent on recognizing our spiritual blindness.

STOP AND SAVOR

Today we focused on this truth: *When we recognize our spiritual blindness, Jesus can open our eyes to see our need for Him.*

> **Summarize your personal takeaway from today's lesson.**

> **What words and/or actions of Jesus stand out most to you in the healing of the blind man? Why?**

> **How has Jesus opened your eyes spiritually?**

PRAYER

Jesus, You are the Healer. Please restore my sight spiritually so that I can see You clearly. Thank You for Your patience with me as You make me aware of blind spots that need attention. Lord, I know I need Your help to see. Shine Your light on the path ahead of me today. In Jesus's name, Amen.

Video Viewer Guide

When we look beneath the surface of our longings, we discover Jesus as our _____ of _____.

"Look beneath the _____ so you can judge _____."

JOHN 7:24, NLT

Only Jesus can quench our _____ _____ (John 7:37-39).

Notes about the Festival of Tabernacles:

-

-

-

"Is anyone _____? Come and drink—even if you have no money! Come, take your choice of wine or milk—it's all free!"

ISAIAH 55:1, NLT

"For my people have done two evil things: They have abandoned me—the fountain of _____ _____. And they have dug for themselves cracked _____ that can hold no water at all!"

JEREMIAH 2:13, NLT

Only Jesus can lift our _____ (John 8:4-11).

Only Jesus can give us _____ _____ (John 8:12).

CHALLENGE FOR THE WEEK: Ask two godly people in your life to tell you if they see anything in your life that could potentially be spiritual blind spots.

(Answers are available on p. 185.)

GROUP DISCUSSION GUIDE

SHARE: How many glasses of water do you typically drink in a day?

WATCH the video "Session Four: Savoring Peace in the Patience of Jesus" together and follow along with the viewer guide on the previous page.

MEMORY VERSE: Review John 7:24 and provide time for group members to recite it aloud.

VIDEO DISCUSSION

1. *Ask:* What longings are typically experienced by women (companionship, purpose, looking better physically, etc.)? What does it mean to look beneath the surface of the longings in your life to find God as your source of satisfaction? Is this easy or difficult for you? Explain.

2. *Discuss:* How does the background information regarding the Festival of Tabernacles provide insight into Jesus's offer of water?

STUDY DISCUSSION

1. *Ask:* Did Jesus's patience with His family, the crowd, or His critics stand out most to you? Explain.

2. Encourage participants to share responses from their answers to the questions in the Stop and Savor section for Day Two on page 79.

3. Call on a volunteer to read aloud John 8:1-11. Discuss every woman's battle with shame. Talk about how this story can help us when we are in the trenches of condemnation— whether from others or self-inflicted.

4. *Ask:* As you evaluate your thoughts, your media choices, and your words, what does God's light of both conviction and hope expose and encourage in your life? (p. 85)

5. Discuss the different lenses that were worn in Day Five and how women can relate to seeing life through criticism, fear, or faith. *Ask:* How do those perspectives impact our peace?

REVIEW the Big Idea for each of the five days of study. Ask for final thoughts or questions regarding the study of God's patience this week.

PRAYER: Acquire a thirty-second hourglass timer (or use the timer on your phone). Allow women to share one specific prayer request before the sand/time runs out. This will help women gather their thoughts and be succinct. It also leaves more time for actual prayer rather than extended sharing of prayer requests.

 To access the video teaching sessions, use the instructions in the back of your Bible study book.

PEACE IN THE

PURPOSES

OF JESUS

THE THIEF'S PURPOSE IS TO
STEAL AND KILL AND DESTROY.
MY PURPOSE IS TO GIVE THEM
A RICH AND SATISFYING LIFE.

John 10:10

Day One
A RICH AND SATISFYING LIFE

SCRIPTURE FOCUS
John 10

BIG IDEA
Jesus is the door to a rich and satisfying life.

Recently my husband was waiting at his office at church to do a premarital counseling meeting with a young couple. He decided to walk outside for some fresh air and sunshine beforehand. Whey they arrived, he led them to the locked entry door, only to realize his keys were on his desk. Together, they walked the perimeter of the building and tried all the doors with no success. Eventually someone arrived and let them in. They laughed together about their minor predicament, but sometimes being locked out can be frustrating or even frightening depending on the situation.

If you can recall a time when you were locked out, describe it in a sentence below.

Today in John 10, we will focus on how Jesus is the door to us experiencing a rich and satisfying life.

ENTERING IN

READ JOHN 10:1-10 and write what you learn about each of these:

The shepherd

Thieves and robbers were classified differently in ancient law. Thieves were criminals who broke in, while robbers were those who lived in the wild and assaulted people passing by.[1]

The sheep

Thieves and robbers

Jesus's purpose

Let's review a few facts about shepherding during the time of Jesus that might help us gain greater understanding as we approach the text:

- Sheep were often herded into a walled enclosure at night to protect them from predators.[2]

- The shepherd's body literally served as the door of the enclosure. He slept across the opening to keep sheep in and predators out.

- Sometimes shepherds combined their flocks into a large fold and had one doorkeeper serve as the gate of protection.[3]

- Near-Eastern shepherds called their own sheep and assembled their flocks with each sheep recognizing the master's particular call.[4]

- Sheep responded to their shepherds' voice but not to the voice of a stranger.[5]

What stands out to you from this information?

Jesus said He is "the gate" (v. 7, CSB, NIV, NLT; or "the door," ESV, NKJV). He is the protector of the sheep and keeps the enemy at bay. He is also the only entrance into His sheepfold. And those who enter His flock will be saved and find freedom, protection, and provision. Jesus, the protecting and providing Good Shepherd, stands in contrast to the thief.

While the thief comes "to steal and kill and destroy" (v. 10), Jesus came to give us life. Perhaps your translation of John 10:10 says "life . . . to the full" (NIV), "life . . . in abundance" (CSB), or "a rich and satisfying life" (NLT). The Greek word that describes life in this verse is *perissos* and means, "exceeding some number or measure or rank or need."[6] Jesus wasn't just talking about giving us a better life experience but giving us life from God found in Him.

Would you say you're experiencing the abundant life that Jesus offers? Why or why not?

The thief metaphor is associated with Satan, whose intent is to destroy rather than preserve life (John 8:44; 1 Pet. 5:8; 1 John 3:8).

Maybe you feel like your difficulties are exceeding your satisfaction. Jesus didn't promise overflowing wealth or material possession. Nor did He promise a perfect or easy life. But He did promise life beyond what we can imagine—life filled with joy, purpose, and meaning, more internal satisfaction rather than external affluence. This fits what we've learned about savoring peace in our journey through John's Gospel; it's more an internal posture, a tranquil state of the soul, than an external state of calm circumstances.

LISTENING TO HIS VOICE

READ JOHN 10:11-21 and record how the Good Shepherd is described versus how the hired hand is described.

GOOD SHEPHERD	HIRED HAND
Verse 11	Verse 12
Verses 14-15	Verse 13

Ezekiel 34 is a passage where God rebukes the "shepherds, the leaders of Israel" (v. 2), the religious leaders in Ezekiel's day who slaughtered the choice animals, clothed themselves in wool, and failed to care for the flock.[7]

While good shepherds serve their flocks in many ways, John emphasized that Jesus came to lay down His life for His sheep. He's not only the Shepherd who leads, He's the Shepherd who serves, sacrificially. That's why we can trust His voice.

It was a rare occurrence for Palestinian shepherds to die in service of sheep. When they did, it was always by accident.[8] Yet, five times in this account Jesus clearly referenced His sacrificial death (John 10:11,15,17-18).

What is the role of sheep according to verses 14 and 16?

Sheep know and listen to their master. They need guidance and protection. In the same way, we need the Good Shepherd to lead us. Without Him we are lost. Yet, too often I listen to the voices of culture, other people, or my own fickle feelings.

Take a moment to evaluate how you are doing at listening to the Good Shepherd's direction in your life. Write your findings below.

To gain a wider view of how the shepherd metaphor has been used throughout Scripture, check out the digging deeper article titled, "Sheep and Shepherds" found online at **lifeway. com/gospelofjohn.**

FOLLOWING HIS VOICE

READ JOHN 10:22-42 and draw a line to match the item in the column on the left with its definition in the column on the right.

Holiday (v. 22)	Solomon's Colonnade/Portico
Location (v. 23)	The works Jesus did in His Father's name
People's question (v. 24)	Stoning
The proof (v. 25)	Listen and follow
Jesus's sheep (v. 27)	Are you the Messiah?
People's response (v. 31)	Festival of Dedication/Hanukkah

The Feast of Dedication (Hanukkah) is not mentioned in the Old Testament, but Jesus celebrated the eight-day festival in the month of December.[9]

The Festival of Dedication commemorated events that took place during the intertestamental period and was the last great deliverance for the Jews. It was a symbol of hope that God would again deliver His people. The Jews awaited a Messiah, but couldn't see how Jesus's works and words revealed His identity as the Son of God.

Let's move this a little closer to home. Take a moment to evaluate your listening life. Record below one small change you could make in your daily rhythms to incorporate more intentional listening to God's voice.

Perhaps you will turn off music or podcasts while on a walk, in the car, or doing household tasks to focus on listening. Maybe you can slow down while reading Scripture to ask Jesus to reveal what He needs you to hear. Whatever your action step is, remember that Jesus calls us to enter in, listen, and follow His voice. He is the door to a rich and satisfying life.

STOP AND SAVOR

Today we focused on this truth: *Jesus is the door to a rich and satisfying life.*

Summarize your personal takeaway from today's lesson.

What characteristics of Jesus as a Shepherd stand out to you and why?

What good things from God can you savor today?

PRAYER

Lord, You are the door, the Good Shepherd, and the Son of God. Help me not to oversaturate my ears with other voices so that I can't hear Yours. Lord, I am Your sheep. I need direction, protection, and provision. Please guide me today. Help me to listen to and follow Your voice. In Jesus's name, Amen.

Day Two
GOD'S GLORY

Our son looked forward to his college graduation in Cincinnati, Ohio, a city he loved and planned to settle in. Then his plans fell apart. He graduated in May 2020, just two months after the whole country had shut down. Most businesses weren't hiring, as they were waiting to see the economic impact of the pandemic. However, a company where he had interned contacted him about an opening in Texas. He interviewed over zoom, was offered the job, and took what seemed like the only option. He missed his church and friends while trying to make connections in a new town. Over the next year he traveled back to Ohio to stand up as a groomsman in five weddings while still not finding his own life partner.

He questioned God and experienced loneliness but leaned into his faith as he sought to find community in his new town.

Can you recall a time when you struggled to understand God's timing in your life, specifically what felt like a delay on His part? If so, jot down a few notes.

SCRIPTURE FOCUS
John 11

BIG IDEA
With God, what feels like a pointless pause to us can have a powerful purpose.

Waiting often seems pointless, even painful at times. Yet God has powerful purposes in pauses.

THE DELAY

READ JOHN 11:1-16 and identify two purposes for Jesus's delay.

Verse 4

Verse 15

Jesus's first of seven signs in the Gospel of John occurred at a wedding, and His last took place at a funeral.

Usually a large group of people— family, friends, and perhaps hired mourners— accompanied a body being taken to the grave. The mourning for the dead usually lasted several days after the burial.[10]

Jesus wasn't aimlessly wandering through His ministry just reacting to the applause of crowds or the threats of the Jewish leaders. He had purpose in all He did. His intentional delay in coming to Lazarus was to bring glory to the Father and lead His disciples to true faith in Him.

Once Jesus expressed His intention to go to Bethany, the disciples protested.

What was their concern according to verse 8?

Lazarus's sickness must have been serious for his sisters to reach out to Jesus. They lived in Bethany, only two miles from Jerusalem. The last time in Jerusalem, Jesus faced the threat of arrest and stoning (John 10:22-39). But this did not deter Him. Jesus didn't operate from fear; He followed the will of His Father.

John's Gospel gives us the best glimpse into Jesus's understanding of His timeline. He was in sync with the Father's purposes. As we consider our own lives, we can savor peace in knowing that God is never late or early.

What good purposes have come out of waiting seasons in your life?

We may encounter seasons when it feels like God didn't show up or allowed something devastating to happen. Even in these times, God can receive glory and our faith can be strengthened as we trust His purposes over what makes sense to us.

THE DECLARATION

READ JOHN 11:17-32 **and summarize what Jesus told Martha in verses 25-26.**

Martha was grieving and struggling to reconcile the death of her brother with the claims of Jesus. Jesus asked her if she believed His words. Not just that she believed in a coming resurrection, but that He is the resurrection. We must also consider what we believe. Does this truth guide the direction and purpose of our lives?

We can savor the peace of Jesus because He is the source of resurrection life. Even in death—our own or those we love—we can savor peace knowing that we pass from earthly life to eternal life if we belong to Jesus.

THE DISPLAY OF EMOTION

READ JOHN 11:33-44 and identify Jesus's emotions in this text.

Why do you think Jesus was troubled?

Let's look at the two Greek words used in verse 33 to better understand Jesus's emotions.

1. The text first says Jesus was "deeply moved in [his] spirit" (CSB, ESV, NIV), "groaned in the spirit" (NKJV), "a deep anger welled up within him" (NLT). This phrase is the Greek word *enebrimesato*, which literally means "to snort like a horse" and "generally connotes anger."[11] Most commentators agree Jesus was not angry at Mary or Martha but at death itself.

2. The text then adds that Jesus was "troubled" (CSB, NIV, NKJV), "deeply troubled" (NLT), "greatly troubled" (ESV), which is translated from the Greek word *etaraxen* which "expresses agitation, confusion, or disorganization."[12] Jesus was not apathetic in the situation. He shared in the common feeling of grief with those He loved.

Jesus knew God's glory and peoples' belief were godly purposes for His delay, but Jesus is as fully human as He is God. Mary wept, the mourners cried, and Jesus entered into their pain. Death angered Him and its painful affects grieved Him. He expressed human emotions, including tears.

What emotions have been surfacing in your life this week?

In what ways do you express your emotions?

I sometimes avoid strong emotions, stuffing them down or trying to reason them away. I've worked with a coach to uncover the roots of my avoidance. Deep inside I believed a lie that anger, crying, or struggling with emotions revealed a lack of faith. I thought true belief would evidence as peace and hope rather than sadness, numbness, or disappointment. This passage validates that feelings themselves aren't sinful or a measure of faith. Give yourself biblical permission to express feelings, whether they are celebratory, apathetic, or overflowing with grief. Just a word of caution: while our feelings aren't sinful, sometimes the way we express them can be. Be careful that your emotional expressions don't present as unwise decisions, hurtful words, or wrong behavior.

Jesus didn't lack faith; He felt and expressed human emotions.

THE DELIBERATIONS

READ JOHN 11:45-57 and record the different responses to Jesus raising Lazarus from the dead.

The Sanhedrin was the supreme court of Israel. They wielded political and spiritual power but remained under Roman authority.[13]

VERSE	PERSON/PEOPLE	RESPONSE
Verse 45	Many people	
Verse 46	Some people	
Verses 47-48	Leading priests and Pharisees	
Verses 49-50	Caiaphas	

VERSE	PERSON/ PEOPLE	RESPONSE
Verse 53	Jewish leaders	

While many people believed that Jesus was the resurrection and the life, others wanted to eliminate Him.

Each of us must decide whether we believe in Jesus.

In John 11, faith was put to the test in a difficult time. Some seasons are harder than others.

My son eventually found friends in his new town, and one day met a girl at church who is now his wife. He would definitely say she was worth the wait! In times when God's pauses seem pointless and even painful, we can lean into the truth that He has powerful purposes for our lives.

STOP AND SAVOR

Today we focused on this truth: *With God, what feels like a pointless pause to us can have a powerful purpose.*

Summarize your personal takeaway from today's lesson.

What do you savor about Jesus from the account of Lazarus's resurrection?

What new perspectives regarding waiting can you embrace based on today's passage?

PRAYER

Jesus, You are the resurrection and my life. Help me trust You in my times of trouble so that I can give You glory. Give me eyes to see Your purposes, especially in seasons when grief overtakes my senses. Be present with me as I feel my feelings. I'm so grateful that You experienced humanity so You can fully understand my pain. In Jesus's name, Amen.

Day Three

DEATH

My friends, Jimmy and Kelly, felt led by God to pursue an international adoption. In preparation for the adoption, Jimmy met with a good friend who had adopted a child under similar circumstances. Jimmy wanted to talk about the potential realities of this decision, including the impact on his marriage, his biological children, and his finances.

His friend didn't sugarcoat it. He told Jimmy he could expect to die to his own desires when it came to things like sleep, entertainment, and purchases. But he reminded him that the gospel is about dying to self.

BIG IDEA
The way to life requires death.

When we pursue gospel obedience, it often feels a little bit like dying—to our comfort, our expectations, and our agendas. As we examine the purposes of Jesus in this week's study, we'll see that for Jesus to be the resurrection and the life, He had to die.

PURPOSE OF PREPARATION

READ JOHN 12:1-11 and match the person with the description.

The man Jesus raised from the dead	Judas Iscariot
The woman serving dinner	Jesus
The woman who anointed Jesus's feet	Leading priests
The disciple who criticized the woman	Mary
The One who said to leave the woman alone	Lazarus
The group of people who wanted to kill Lazarus	Martha

What details stood out to you from this text?

In Jesus's day, it was not uncommon to spend lavishly for a funeral, including the cost of perfumes to hide the smell of decay.[14] But Mary was pouring out an expensive fragrance on Jesus while He was still alive. Jesus knew Mary's deed had great purpose—she was symbolically preparing Him for His death.

The cost of the perfume would have been an enormous sum—equivalent to a year's wages. Either Mary and her family were wealthy or the perfume could have been a family heirloom.[15]

Sometimes circumstances in our lives can be puzzling. Can you look back and see how a particular circumstance, perhaps even a painful one, served a greater purpose in your life? If so, jot a note about it below.

I remember when a conflict with close friends revealed patterns of gossip and selfishness in my life. It wasn't a fun season, but it led me to repentance and a more intimate walk with the Lord. Difficult circumstances can be a catalyst that leads us to die to self in order to live to God. God's purposes in our circumstances are not to harm us. Rather, He leads us to die to self so that we may discover a rich and satisfying life in close relationship with Him.

PURPOSE OF PEACE

READ JOHN 12:12-19 and either sketch the scene or describe it in your own words below.

The triumphal entry of Jesus into Jerusalem is one of the few events recorded in all four Gospels (Matt. 21:1-11; Mark 11:1-11; Luke 19:29-38).

John quoted Zechariah 9:9-10, which foretold the Messiah riding on a donkey. The prophecy also detailed the king as humble and peaceful, destroying weapons rather than building an army.

The crowds wanted a warrior king but Jesus's entrance made it clear that was not His purpose at this time. By riding in on a donkey, Jesus presented Himself as one coming in peace, not to lead the people in a revolt against Rome. This type of entrance would serve to quell any "nationalistic expectations."[16]

Peace wasn't coming in the way the disciples, the crowd, or the religious leaders expected. They wanted political peace. Jesus was bringing peace with God.

The peace Jesus brings comes in unexpected ways in our lives as well. Sometimes we experience peace just by recognizing our need for God in the midst of grief, conflict, or unmet expectations. Through disruption we often see beyond earthly circumstances to heavenly priorities.

In what ways has Jesus brought unexpected peace into your life?

PURPOSE IN SUFFERING

The Greeks were likely God-fearing Gentiles who came to worship at the Feast of the Passover. It's possible they approached Philip because he had a Greek name.[17]

READ JOHN 12:20-36 and write contrasting statements to the statements listed in the following verses. (I did the first one for you.)

VERSE(S)	STATEMENT	CONTRASTING STATEMENT
Verse 24	An unplanted seed remains alone.	The death of the seed produces new life.
Verse 25	Those who love their lives will lose it.	

VERSE(S)	STATEMENT	CONTRASTING STATEMENT
Verses 27-28	Father, save me from this hour.	
Verse 35	Those who walk in darkness can't see where they're going.	

Jesus used several illustrations to help His listeners understand the purpose of His suffering and death. In a farming society, planting and harvesting would have been familiar to the whole community. Jesus pointed out that a seed is weak and useless until it dies. Only then does it fulfill its purpose.

John repeated the contrast of light and darkness throughout his Gospel (John 1:4-9; 3:19-21; 8:12; 12:35-36,46).

Throughout John's account, Jesus has been saying that His hour had not yet come. However, when the Greeks asked for an audience with Jesus, He signaled that His hour had come. He was deeply troubled by it because He knew His purpose in coming: He came to die.

Despite the agony ahead, Jesus trusted that His death would be a doorway to life. When we choose to follow Christ, we understand gospel purposes are not accomplished by loving this life. This isn't self-hatred but turning our attention to something bigger than just the pleasures of today.

Jesus taught that the way to real life is death. Jimmy's friend from our opening story reminds us that hard things are hard but worth it. If it doesn't feel a little bit like dying, it may not be the gospel.

PURPOSE OF BELIEF

READ JOHN 12:37-50. What did Jesus say was His purpose (v. 46)?

Jesus told the crowd that trusting Him was trusting God. But despite seeing the miracles, many hardened their hearts in unbelief. Others did believe but feared the repercussions from the Pharisees, so they didn't commit to follow Him. They had a superficial rather than a sincere belief. Jesus doesn't force Himself on anyone, but He invites each of us to believe in Him.

How is Jesus calling you to trust Him more fully in the midst of your current circumstances?

Jesus's purpose was not accomplished without His death. Our calling is also contingent on our willingness to die—to deny ourselves and give up our lives to follow. In this we will discover real life as we live for Him.

STOP AND SAVOR

Today we focused on this truth: *The way to life requires death.*

Summarize your personal takeaway from today's lesson.

What of Jesus's words and interactions stood out to you and why?

How does today's lesson help you savor the peace of Jesus?

Day Four
SERVING

Summer after summer I was blown away by the college students who served at family camp. They valet-parked our van, unloaded our luggage, and seemed to enjoy pouring our kids' drinks at meals. I watched them do the most menial tasks with genuine delight.

What are some ways you have served others, and how has that spiritually energized you?

How have others served you, and how has their service been a blessing to you?

Serving can take many shapes—like mowing a neighbor's lawn, tending a sick family member, or holding babies in the church nursery. For Jesus, it included washing dirty feet.

HUMILITY

READ JOHN 13:1-5 and fill in the blanks:
- This happened before the _____ celebration.
- Jesus knew that His _____ had come to leave this world.
- Jesus knew His _____ had given Him authority to come to earth and now return to heaven.
- Jesus got up from the table and began to _____ His disciples' feet.

Chapter 13 begins what scholars refer to as Jesus's farewell discourse (John 13–17). In these first five verses we see that Jesus wasn't a victim of circumstances. He clearly understood the decisive end to His public

SCRIPTURE FOCUS
John 13:1-17

BIG IDEA
Jesus came to serve, and we can savor peace in following His example.

A farewell discourse was a well-established biblical pattern. Some other biblical examples include Jacob's blessing of his children (Gen. 47:29–49:33), Joshua's goodbye to Israel (Josh. 22–24) and David's farewell speech (1 Chron. 28–29).[18]

ministry initiated the sequence of events leading up to the cross. The unbelieving crowds were gone, and Jesus reemphasized His love for His disciples. They would be the focus of His final teachings.

How do you see Jesus's humility lived out in verse 5?

This was a private gathering so it's likely no servants were on hand to wash feet. None of the disciples volunteered to perform what was considered a lowly task. In fact, Luke informs us that the disciples were arguing over who would be the greatest in the kingdom of God as they sat at the table (Luke 22:24). Jesus's wordless, humble gesture would have rebuked their attitudes. Also, His washing of feet was much more significant than merely meeting an immediate need. This act foreshadowed the cross—the selfless service Jesus exhibited to the point of death.

HOLINESS

READ JOHN 13:6-11 and write your personal impressions of Peter's protests and Jesus's responses below.

I love how Peter is an all-or-nothing kind of guy. He initially opposed Jesus degrading Himself but then wanted an entire scrubbing. It's clear Peter didn't quite fathom what Jesus was doing. That's understandable, since even today scholars disagree on the meaning of Jesus's words. The way I see it, Jesus used the washing of feet as an illustration of sanctifying spiritual cleansing.

Salvation isn't just a past experience; it's also a present reality. We have been saved from the penalty of sin (justification), we are being saved from the power of sin (sanctification), and we will be saved from the presence of sin (glorification). This picture of washing dirty feet is about holy living—sanctification—the daily process of growing in Christ as we walk in this world. We have an ongoing need for confession, repentance, and refreshing because of our continual struggle with sin, even after we've been saved. We don't need to be saved over and over again because our relationship with God through Christ is eternally secure. We just need cleansing restoration when we break fellowship with the Lord.

Jesus knew Peter would betray Him and get His feet dirty again and again. He would fail at critical moments. This washing of feet would provide hope on the other side of failure.

Where do you need cleansing today in your struggle with the power of sin? What keeps getting your feet dirty?

These verses give me hope that Jesus knows about my dirty feet. He understands my bent toward sin but washes me and gives me the power to change. We will never be sinless this side of heaven, but by receiving His cleansing He restores us and reminds us of His power in us to sin less as we mature in our relationship with Him.

How does Peter's dialogue with Jesus give you hope as you consider your own sanctification process?

HELPING

READ JOHN 13:12-17 and record Jesus's instructions in verses 14-15 in your own words.

John chose not to include the details of the communion elements but to focus on the foot washing part of the last supper. Perhaps John had nothing to add to what the other three Gospel writers had covered or chose to highlight Jesus's humility and holiness.

Though the disciples were focused on the levels of their greatness, Jesus showed that following Him meant not being above the lowest job. Not much has changed when it comes to people seeking greatness over humility. But Jesus set the tone of servant leadership for every one of us who claim Him as Savior. We are not here to be served but to serve.

As you reflect on Jesus's example and command regarding serving, consider where you are currently serving in your family, church, community, etc., and list a few examples below:

- _____

- _____

- _____

I've filled in those blanks differently over the years. Some years I would have written "changing diapers, helping with homework, and meal prep." Currently, I mentor a student at my local high school, lead a Bible study, and serve family members and friends as needed.

Consider your posture toward the opportunities you listed. Write a word or phrase beside each one that describes your attitude in carrying out the task.

Consider the following questions and ask the Lord to prompt you by His Spirit with any action steps you need to take. Jot a note following each one if you sense any direction.

Is the Lord calling you to make an attitude adjustment when it comes to serving? If so, in what way?

What needs have you noticed around you (home, church, community, etc.) that you could meet?

Serving can be about as glamorous as washing dirty feet, but it can be a vehicle on the road to fulfilling our God-given purpose. Two of my children have now served as staffers at the family camp I mentioned in the opening paragraph. They would tell you those seasons of serving were physically exhausting but spiritually enriching. Often, we seek peace through entertainment or consuming more stuff, but it never ultimately satisfies. Jesus says we will be fulfilled as we pour out our lives in humility, holiness, and helping others.

STOP AND SAVOR

Today we focused on this truth: *Jesus came to serve, and we can savor peace in following His example.*

Summarize your personal takeaway from today's lesson.

What stands out to you about Jesus's words and actions from today's Scripture?

What is one tangible way you can serve someone today? How will that help you savor the peace of Jesus?

Day Five

LOVE

SCRIPTURE FOCUS

John 13:18-35

Our culture is in love with love. We love pizza. We love comfy clothes. We love our friends. If we aren't careful, the word *love* can fall prey to overuse that robs the word of its significance.

How would you define *love*?

BIG IDEA

Jesus teaches us to love and be loved.

Maybe you said something like strong admiration or unconditional affection. The Greek word for "love" we will encounter in today's text is *agapao,* one of several Greek words for love. It's a verb that "refers to a pure, willful, sacrificial love that intentionally desires another's highest good."[19] That's not something we feel about food or fads, but a love we supernaturally receive from God and share with others.

As we close out our week of study focused on savoring peace in the purposes of Jesus, we will find no greater purpose than love. Jesus loved His disciples and commands us to love as He loved.

The usual arrangement at a meal in Jesus's day was to have a series of couches forming a U-shape around a low table with the host placed at the center and the most honored guests on His immediate right and left side.[20]

LOVING ALL THE WAY

READ JOHN 13:18-30 **and answer the following questions:**

Why did Jesus tell the disciples about His betrayer ahead of time (v. 19)?

What emotion did Jesus experience as He anticipated His betrayal (v. 21)?

After Judas ate, what pace did Jesus encourage him to take (v. 27)?

We saw in the previous day of study that Jesus washed the disciples' dirty feet, including those of Judas. Many scholars suggest that Judas may have been seated in the place of honor on Jesus's left since Jesus was able to speak to him privately.[21] So, Jesus honored Judas, possibly with a special seat and certainly by offering him the morsel of bread.[22] While Judas received the food, he did not receive the love. Instead, he quickly proceeded into literal and spiritual darkness.

Jesus loved even those who opposed Him. We should follow His example in loving all the way.

What is a practical way you can show love to someone with whom you have a complicated relationship?

AN IDENTITY OF LOVE

RE-READ JOHN 13:23. **How is the person sitting next to Jesus at the table described? Who do you think this is?**

This is the first mention of the "beloved disciple," who most scholars agree is John, the author of this Gospel. This description will be repeated at the cross (19:26-27), the empty tomb (20:2), the Sea of Tiberias when Jesus appeared in resurrected body (21:20), and implied in the final two verses of the book (21:24-25).

Why John described himself in that way is unknown. But we do know John understood and received the love that motivated God to send Jesus (John 3:16). John wasn't displaying arrogance. Instead, he was likely expressing his indebtedness to grace. One commentator said the description was John's "quiet way of refusing to give even the impression of sharing a platform with Jesus."[23]

Jesus transformed John's life, and John wanted to give Him all the glory. In the same way, God has changed our lives, and we can now see ourselves as loved by God, even though we don't always feel loved. My dad died from Stage 4 cancer during the writing of this study.

I remember when we first got the news, I often found myself troubled and crying from grief. But like Jesus, who knew He was loved by the Father even as He moved toward the cross of suffering, we can identify ourselves as loved by God as we endure difficulties like cancer, sorrow, and death.

> **Take a moment to remember who and whose you are. Write your name in the blanks below. Then meditate on these truths:**
>
> **_____ is loved by God. Jesus suffered and died to give His life for _____ in order to restore her relationship with the Father.**

If you have committed your life to Jesus, you are His beloved disciple. John understood his position, and we can too. We are loved.

LOVING AS JESUS LOVED

Jesus showed us how to love. He loved Judas, and He also loved His disciples by preparing them as best He could for what was to come. The disciples would have been disoriented by Jesus's predictions about His coming suffering and betrayal, especially in light of His miracles which brought popularity and crowds. They couldn't fully appreciate what Jesus knew was coming.

> **READ JOHN 13:31-38. Explain Jesus's new commandment in your own words.**

Leviticus 19:18 would have been a familiar verse to Jesus's disciples, "Do not seek revenge or bear a grudge against a fellow Israelite, but love your neighbor as yourself. I am the LORD."

> **In your opinion, what could be considered "new" about Jesus's commandment to love?**

The command to "love each other" in John 13:34 was not new. But while the law instructed people to love each other as they love themselves, Jesus's new command is for us to love others the way He loved us. This wasn't possible until God dwelt among us and sent His Spirit to dwell in us.

Jesus said this kind of love for one another would prove to the world that we are His disciples. John wrote more about this in 1 John 4:

> If someone says, "I love God," but hates a fellow believer, that person is a liar; for if we don't love people we can see, how can we love God, whom we cannot see? And he has given us this command: Those who love God must also love their fellow believers.
> 1 JOHN 4:20-21

In what way is the Holy Spirit prompting you concerning how you love your brothers and sisters in Christ? Are you truly loving them as Jesus loves you? Are there new relationships you need to deepen? Broken ones you need to mend? Write below what comes to mind as you listen to the Lord.

We can't love others like Jesus without Jesus. Let's savor His love now and commit to sharing it abundantly.

STOP AND SAVOR

Today we focused on this truth: *Jesus teaches us to love and be loved.*

Summarize your personal takeaway from today's lesson.

What words and actions of Jesus stand out to you today, and why?

How does savoring the peace of Jesus enhance our ability to love like Him?

PRAYER

Jesus, I am Your beloved disciple. Please help me to see myself as You see me. Sometimes loving others can be challenging. You know my struggles. Fill me so full with Your love that it overflows to everyone, even the people I find hard to love. In Jesus's name, Amen.

Video Viewer Guide

Jesus's _____ are always good, even when our
_____ aren't.

Jesus didn't come to give you a _____ life. He came to give
you an _____ life (John 10:9-11).

"The LORD is my _____;
I have all that I _____."

PSALM 23:1, NLT

The Shepherd's concern is _____; a sheep's concern
is _____ to the Shepherd's voice (John 10:27).

We spend a lot of energy trying to _____ things we
can't control.

When we see no _____ purpose, we trust the _____
_____ purpose (John 11:33,35,38).

Two questions to ask:

• How can I _____ God through this pain?

• How can I _____ that Jesus is the Resurrection and
the Life even as I lament?

CHALLENGE FOR THE WEEK: Add two minutes of listening after
you complete each day of study next week. Use the time to reflect,
ask questions, and listen quietly.

(Answers are available on p. 185.)

GROUP DISCUSSION GUIDE

SHARE: What music, podcasts, or videos have you been listening to or watching this week?

WATCH the video "Session Five: Savoring Peace in the Purposes of Jesus" together and follow along with the viewer guide on the previous page.

MEMORY VERSE: Review John 10:10 and provide time for group members to recite it aloud.

VIDEO DISCUSSION

1. *Ask:* What resonated most as you watched the teaching? Why?
2. *Discuss:* What are some practical ways to let go of controlling behaviors and trust Jesus as your Good Shepherd?

STUDY DISCUSSION

1. Call on a volunteer to read aloud John 10:1-10. Discuss correlations between a shepherd's role and Jesus's care for us.
2. *Ask:* What good purposes have come out of waiting seasons in your life? (p. 102)
3. Discuss participants answers to the questions in the Stop and Savor section for Day Three on page 110.
4. Call on a volunteer to read aloud John 13:1-5. Ask: What are some ways you have served others, and how has that spiritually energized you? (p. 111)
5. *Ask:* What insights about loving one another did you glean from Day Five?

REVIEW the Big Idea for each of the five days of study. Ask for final thoughts or questions regarding the study of God's purposes this week.

PRAYER: Close with a "popcorn prayer." Encourage group members to say a word or phrase of praise to God. Then lead women to use a word or brief phrases to express specific requests to the Lord. As the leader, close the prayer time.

To access the video teaching sessions, use the instructions in the back of your Bible study book.

PEACE IN THE
PROMISES
OF JESUS

I AM LEAVING YOU WITH A GIFT—

PEACE OF MIND AND HEART.

AND THE PEACE I GIVE IS A GIFT

THE WORLD CANNOT GIVE.

SO DON'T BE TROUBLED OR AFRAID.

John 14:27

Day One
PROMISES IN TROUBLED TIMES

SCRIPTURE FOCUS

John 14:1-14

BIG IDEA

You can savor peace as you consider where you'll go, Who you know, and what Jesus bestows.

One commentator said a good translation of Jesus's command in John 14:1 would be, "Set your heart at ease."[1]

As I mentioned earlier in the study, my father battled late-stage cancer before passing away. I remember it being such a rough season. I know hopeful truths about Jesus and resurrection life after death, yet in the same breath my heavy heart leads to tears when I reflect on that time. I miss my dad, and I mourn for my mom, who is alone after fifty-three years of marriage.

I find comfort and see God's kindness to me personally as together we focus this week on savoring peace in the promises of Jesus in John 14–17. In these chapters, Jesus shares promises we can stand on whether we are encountering a season of intense difficulty, incredible celebration, or anything in between. We will also discover that persecution and pruning can benefit our souls.

READ JOHN 14:1 and write Jesus's instruction below.

Jesus calls us to trust Him and the Father. But how we can accomplish that, particularly when we experience difficult circumstances?

Has something been troubling your heart lately? If so, write a few words about it.

Perhaps you're dealing with a sick child, an irritating family member, or a bill that's due soon. We don't need to minimize our troubles just because someone else's seems bigger. Our pain is our pain. Jesus knew what trouble felt like, even before the cross. When His friend Lazarus died and Judas betrayed Him, we read that Jesus was troubled. He understands human emotion because He "became human and made his home among us" (John 1:14).

Jesus also knew His disciples were troubled. He had just revealed that one of them would betray Him (13:21) and that He was leaving them (v. 33).

Certainly, Peter would have been disturbed by the news that he would deny Jesus three times before the night was over (v. 38). Yet, He told them not to let their hearts be troubled.

Jesus was saying you don't have to let your feelings boss you around. You can lament, but anxiety doesn't get the final word. Instead, you can savor peace as you consider where you'll go, Who you know, and what prayer bestows.

WHERE YOU'LL GO

READ JOHN 14:2-3. Where did Jesus says His followers will go?

Scripture uses many descriptions to speak of the next life, including "the eternal Kingdom" (2 Pet. 1:11), "an inheritance" (1 Pet. 1:4), and "a city" (Heb. 11:16). But I love how Jesus described it as "home" (John 14:2).

What are some sights, sounds, or smells that make you think of home?

"The focus of this text is not merely the place but the person; as Jesus said, each Christian will dwell in 'my Father's house.'"[2]

My slippers, cozy blanket, and a cup of tea in my favorite mug all come to my mind.

Jesus said He was preparing a place for us to be with Him forever. Keeping this in perspective gives us hope in the midst of suffering. Measuring our current problems against the hope of heaven allows us to reframe our circumstances with a new mindset.

How does thinking about where you'll go in the next life brighten your outlook today?

I'm still shedding tears knowing my dad has left this earth, but thinking about him forever dwelling in the Father's house brings me peace to savor in the midst of grief.

WHO YOU KNOW

READ JOHN 14:4-11 and circle your answer to the following questions.

Which disciple admitted he had no idea where Jesus was going (v. 5)?

    A.   Philip

    B.   Peter

    C.   Thomas

How did Jesus respond to his question (v. 6)?

    A.   I am the Bread of Life.

    B.   I am the Way, the Truth, and the Life.

    C.   I am the Light of the world.

How did Jesus explain His connection with the Father (vv. 7-11)?

    A.   If you really know me, you know the Father.

    B.   If you have seen me, you have seen the Father.

    C.   I am in the Father, and the Father is in me.

    D.   The words I speak are not my own but from the Father who is in me.

    E.   All of the above.

I love that Thomas voiced what other disciples might have been thinking. Jesus had withdrawn at times to escape arrest. It's possible Thomas thought Jesus was referring to one of those secret places.[3] Bottom line, Thomas didn't know where Jesus was going or how to get there. Jesus responded with another I AM statement, making it clear that the way is a Person. He is the Way.

We don't have to let our hearts be troubled because of Who we know. Jesus made it clear that He and the Father are inseparable. When we know, see, and hear Jesus, we are knowing, seeing, and hearing the Father. He is our Way, our Truth, and our Life.

WHAT JESUS BESTOWS

READ JOHN 14:12-14 and fill in the blanks below. (Answers may vary according to your translation.)

Anyone who believes in Jesus will do _____
_____ **(v. 12).**

Ask for anything in Jesus's name, and He _____
(vv. 13-14).

(Answers: C, B, E)

Jesus invited His followers to ask for anything. He wasn't teaching that we can name and claim our desires, then He delivers like a magic genie. The text qualifies our asking—in Jesus's name. This doesn't mean we can just tack those words onto any prayer and get what we want. Jesus's name represents His character. Asking in His name means asking in line with His will.

What's striking here is the access. Jesus invites us and has made a way for us to converse with the God of creation. Through prayer, Jesus bestows on us an avenue to intimacy with God.

How has talking to Jesus brought you peace when you felt troubled?

My season of grief has been full of tears, but it's also given me a nearness to the Lord that only desperation can bring. Jesus's invitation to ask Him for anything has been a precious gift to me as I've cried out for comfort, grace, and His presence. As we pray, Jesus bestows the power not to let trouble overwhelm us. The next time anxiety knocks at the door of our hearts, we can let prayer answer it![4]

STOP AND SAVOR

Today we focused on this truth: *You can savor peace as you consider where you'll go, who You know, and what Jesus bestows.*

Summarize your personal takeaway from today's lesson.

What stood out to you as you thought about heaven today?

How does Jesus's statement "I am the way, the truth, and the life" in John 14:6 encourage you?

PRAYER

Lord, You are the Way, the Truth, and the Life. It blows my mind that You invite me to ask for anything. Help me to know what to ask for. Align me to Your will so that I bring You glory. Help me see my troubles through the lens of where I'll go, Who I know, and all that You bestow! In Jesus's name, Amen.

Day Two

THE PROMISE OF THE HOLY SPIRIT

SCRIPTURE FOCUS

John 14:15-31

BIG IDEA

Jesus never guaranteed peaceful circumstances but promised to send an Advocate to help us receive His gift of peace.

One evening around the dinner table, our family shared high and low points of the day. One of our twins, who was in third grade at the time, broke into tears as she shared her "low." A teacher had made a comment about her in front of other students that hurt her feelings. My husband asked if she wanted him to speak to the teacher about it. She nodded yes through her tears.

My husband knew that her teacher, a young man new to his profession, likely had little experience with the sensitivities of eight-year-old girls. He kindly took the teacher aside the next morning and mentioned our daughter's hurt feelings. The teacher acknowledged that he was only teasing but could see the impact of his words in the moment and wasn't sure how to handle it. He apologized to our daughter later that day.

> **Can you think of a time when you longed for someone to come to your defense? If so, explain.**

We all need support, particularly when we feel sad, alone, or confused. The disciples certainly found themselves troubled as Jesus continued His farewell discourse around the table at the Last Supper. He spoke of difficult days ahead but also promised them an Advocate to help them.

John 14–17 includes the longest teaching anywhere in Scripture concerning the ministry of the Holy Spirit, including why God sent Him and what He does in our midst.[5]

DEFENDER

READ JOHN 14:15-17 and write at least three things you discover about the Holy Spirit.

1.

2.

3.

In this passage, we encounter a Greek word for "the Holy Spirit" unique to John's Gospel—*parakletos*. It's translated "Advocate," "Counselor" or "Comforter," but literally means "a person summoned to one's aid."[6]

Notice that Jesus said He would give us *another* Advocate. (The Greek word translated "another" means "another of the same kind."[7]) That caused me to wonder about the identity of the other One.

READ 1 JOHN 2:1 below and circle the identity of the first Advocate.

> My dear children, I am writing this to you so that you will not sin. But if anyone does sin, we have an advocate who pleads our case before the Father. He is Jesus Christ, the one who is truly righteous.

Jesus is our Advocate, speaking to the Father in our defense. The Holy Spirit—who is not a force, but a person—would be an advocate, or helper, like Jesus.

How is the Holy Spirit an advocate, helper, and comforter for you?

To see how the Holy Spirit was active in the Old Testament compared to how He works in New Testament believers, check out the digging deeper article titled, "The Holy Spirit" found online at lifeway. com/gospelofjohn.

REMINDERS

READ JOHN 14:18-26 and draw a line from the beginning of the statement on the left to the correct ending on the right.

I will not abandon you as orphans	love me.
Those who obey (keep) my commandments	do what I say.
Anyone (all) who loves me will	teach and remind you of what I said.
The Holy Spirit will	I will come to you.

"The uncompromising connection between love for Christ and obedience to Christ repeatedly recurs in John's writings (*cf.* vv. 21,23; 15:14)."[8]

What did Jesus seem to be emphasizing to His disciples?

Jesus repeatedly connected love and obedience. These strong words can make us uncomfortable. After all, none of us obey all the commandments all the time. Yes, we love Jesus and yet we struggle with sin. But it's not just about following the rules. Take the Pharisees. Their focus was on following all the laws, but Jesus was in constant conflict with them.

Jesus's teaching in John 14 reveals that if our obedience is lacking, we shouldn't try harder to obey. Instead, we should stoke the fires of love and faith. This is the path to peace.

Ask the Holy Spirit to reveal where your love for the Lord might need to be rekindled. What spiritual disciplines or practices would add fuel to the fire? What kinds of attitudes, thinking patterns, or actions are quenching the flames? You don't have to write anything down, just take a minute to ask the Advocate to guide you into greater awareness and deeper love.

"The *pax Romana* ('Roman peace') was won and maintained by a brutal sword; not a few Jews thought the messianic peace would have to be secured by a still mightier sword. Instead, it was secured by an innocent man who suffered and died at the hands of the Romans, of the Jews, and of all of us."[11]

RECEIVERS

READ JOHN 14:27-31 and describe the gift Jesus said He was leaving us.

We've already mentioned the Greek word for "peace" is *eirene*, which means "the tranquil state of a soul assured of its salvation through Christ, and so fearing nothing from God and content with its earthly lot."[9] Though the New Testament is written in Greek these Jewish disciples would have been familiar with the Hebrew word for "peace"—*shalom*. This peace means "completeness, soundness, welfare, peace."[10]

Have you struggled to find peace lately? If so, in what way?

Although Jesus gives us His peace, we don't always walk in it. Too often we're distracted by the world and focused on the storms. What are some practical things you can do to stay centered on Christ and savor His peace?

Chaos is constant in this world until Jesus returns, but it doesn't have to be constant inside us. Instead, we can listen to our Advocate who reminds us of what Jesus promised and receive His peace!

STOP AND SAVOR

Today we focused on this truth: *Jesus never guaranteed peaceful circumstances but promised to send an Advocate to help us receive His gift of peace.*

Summarize your personal takeaway from today's lesson.

From Jesus's teaching on the Holy Spirit, what stands out most to you?

How have you been savoring Jesus's gift of peace lately?

PRAYER

Jesus, thank You for sending the Advocate, the Holy Spirit, to live inside me. Help me believe all that You said and grow deeper in my understanding of Your Spirit. Guide me, remind me of truth, and show me how to receive the gift of peace. I don't want to keep looking for peace from worldly things when You clearly said I won't find it there! In Jesus's name, Amen.

Day Three

A PROMISE TO PRODUCE

**SCRIPTURE
FOCUS**
John 15

This morning I woke up before the alarm on my phone went off. I reached over to see the time and noticed a low battery message. That seemed odd because it appeared to be plugged in. I removed the cord from the phone port and reattached it. It worked! The lightning bolt in the upper right-hand corner appeared indicating it was now charging. Seems a loose connection had been the culprit. Cell phones need regular access to a power source to recharge the battery. Without that proper connection, it can't provide communication, notifications, and information.

BIG IDEA
We need to hang in there with Jesus so He can produce spiritual fruit in our lives.

What other devices you use regularly need to be plugged into a power source to perform?

When the electricity goes out, we discover just how reliant we are on our kitchen appliances, laptops, and hair dryers in everyday life! Today, in John, we pick up the text as Jesus and the disciples had just left the upper room where they ate the last supper. They likely walked toward the Kidron Valley with Jesus teaching along the way.

PROMISE TO PRUNE

READ JOHN 15:1-8 and note who each phrase describes by using the following letters. (Some answers have more than one letter.)

J - Jesus   F - Father   D - Disciples of Jesus

_____ The true vine (v. 1)

_____ The gardener (vinedresser, husbandman) (v. 1)

_____ Cuts off unproductive branches and prunes productive branches (v. 2)

_____ Pruned and cleansed by Jesus's message (v. 3)

_____ Remains or abides (v. 4)

_____ The branches (v. 5)

_____ Apart from Christ, they can do nothing (v. 5)

_____ If they remain in Christ, and His words remain in them, they can ask for anything and receive it (v. 7)

_____ Produce much fruit and bring glory to Him (v. 8)

Jesus revealed His last I AM statement recorded in the book of John: "I am the true grapevine" (John 15:1).

There is rich history in the Scripture with the vine imagery. In the Old Testament, Israel was referred to as the vine (Ps. 80:8-18; Isa. 5:1-7; Jer. 2:21; Ezek. 15:1-5). But for the most part, in these passages, Israel is being chastised for not producing fruit. Then Jesus used the vine as an illustration in His teaching (Matt. 20:1-7; Mark 12:1-11). But here in John 15:1, Jesus declared that He is "the true grapevine" and we are the branches.

What spiritual truths about your relationship with God emerge from this gardening illustration?

The Father watched over the vine, tending and pruning it to secure fruitfulness. Pruning in New Testament times was done with a small hook during winter months. The gardener cut away weak, broken, or diseased branches so the vine could produce the finest grapes possible.[12] Just as unprofitable wood on a plant diverts resources from fruit production, unproductive distractions can inhibit our production of spiritual fruit.

What might the Father prune out of a believer's life in order to produce more fruit? What has He pruned out of yours in the past?

Certainly, the Father wants to cut away sinful things, but other times He may remove good things that have become distractions to growth. It could be a job, relationship, habit, ministry, and so forth. At the time of removal, we often experience pain and possibly confusion. But we can trust that our heavenly Gardener is lovingly allowing pain with purpose.

THE PROMISE OF FRUIT

Jesus promised if we remain in Him we would produce much fruit. He also said that apart from abiding in Him, we could accomplish nothing. We can do a lot of good things on our own, but without His supernatural power, they won't amount to anything in His kingdom.

What does it mean for us to abide or remain in Christ and Christ in us? What does that look like on a practical basis in your relationship with Him?

The Greek word for "abide" or "remain" is *meno*, which means "to continue to be present."[13] *Meno* is used eleven times in the first eleven verses of John 15. We all have a tendency toward self-reliance. Using the vine illustration, Jesus tells us to hang with Him—to stay connected to Him. When we are tempted to stop praying, studying His Word, or any of the other spiritual rhythms that connect us to God, He tells us to continue to show up. When we do, He will supply the power we need to produce fruit.

How would you define *spiritual fruit*?

In the Old Testament, fruit sometimes illustrated offspring (Hos. 9:16) and other times consequences (Prov. 1:31; Isa. 3:10; Jer. 6:19). Paul told the Galatians that the fruit produced in our lives when we yield to the Holy Spirit is godly character—love, peace, patience, and so forth (Gal. 5:22-23). Also in the New Testament, fruit is seen as "praise to God" (Heb. 13:15), meeting needs (Rom. 15:28), and leading people to Christ (Rom. 1:13; Col. 1:6).[14] So basically, our connection to the Vine will be evident by the fruit of character and influence. If we lack evidence of this fruit, we shouldn't beat ourselves up, strive harder, or give up. Instead, we can ask the Lord for help in reconnecting and remaining with Him.

PROMISE OF JOY

READ JOHN 15:9-17. **Summarize what Jesus said about joy in verse 11.**

When we abide with Him, Jesus said our joy will overflow. He wasn't talking about a feeling of happiness based on circumstances. He was talking about a sense of joy that is present even in the midst of grief, disappointment, and difficulties. Like peace, joy runs deeper than circumstances because it rests on God's character.

PROMISE OF PERSECUTION

READ JOHN 15:18-27. From this passage, how you would explain to a teenager the world's hatred for Christians?

Jesus doesn't want us to be caught off guard. The world rejected Him, so they will reject His followers. Knowing this ahead of time means less confusion and disillusionment. Chaos may seem to rule, but Jesus is the Logos, the Living Word, who brings order out of the chaos. The illustration of the vine shows us that, despite what we face as Christians, we can live God-honoring, fruitful lives if we remain in Him.

STOP AND SAVOR

Today we focused on this truth: *We need to hang in there with Jesus so He can produce spiritual fruit in our lives.*

Summarize your personal takeaway from today's lesson.

Which promise from Jesus in John 15 stands out most to you today? Why?

What spiritual disciplines or practices help you continue to remain in Jesus? How can you engage in these more often?

PRAYER

Jesus, sometimes I struggle to remain in You. Please prune from my life things that stifle my spiritual growth. Give me faith to trust this possibly painful work You are doing. I long to abide with You, especially when life is confusing and difficult. Thank You for remaining in me and for the Advocate who reveals Your truth in this chaotic world. In Jesus's name, Amen.

Day Four

PROMISE OF PEACE

SCRIPTURE FOCUS

John 16

BIG IDEA

Jesus promised peace in the midst of chaos through His Spirit and prayer.

My best friend is a math teacher. Just today she was explaining to me how teaching difficult topics has to be done slowly. For example, the Pythagorean theorem for seventh graders requires starting with basics, repeating prior concepts of algebra, and breaking down information into smaller bites.

As I was researching today's study on John 16, I couldn't help but think of my friend's approach of going slow, explaining a little at a time, anticipating questions, and repeating herself. Jesus was in the middle of a marathon teaching loaded with difficult concepts. He had little time left and wanted to help His disciples understand the coming suffering while encouraging them to hold onto the big picture of the Father's love. He promised peace in the midst of chaos through His Spirit and prayer.

READ JOHN 16:1-4 and write the difficulties Jesus described.

Can you imagine learning you will be kicked out of your church and killed by someone who thinks they're serving God by doing so? In discussing these difficult, unpeaceful situations, Jesus employed the method of my math teacher friend to teach, remind, and encourage His followers.

THE SPIRIT OF TRUTH

READ JOHN 16:5-15 and find four specific ways the Holy Spirit advocates for us:

1. He will _____ (v. 8).

2. He will _____ (v. 13a).

3. He will tell you about the _____ (v. 13b).

4. He will bring Jesus glory by _____

_____ (v. 14).

Let's consider how these promises from Jesus regarding the Holy Spirit intersect with our lives today.

1. CONVICT THE WORLD OF SIN, RIGHTEOUSNESS, AND JUDGMENT. The verb *convict* (*elencho*) is a legal term that means to pronounce a judicial verdict. A court can convict a man of murder, but only the Spirit can convict a person of unbelief, as only He can judge motives. If you know Christ, you have experienced the Holy Spirit's conviction, enabling you to recognize your sin and turn from it.

> **When did you first sense the Holy Spirit convicting you of sin? What was that experience like and how did you respond?**

> **Are you experiencing the Spirit's conviction today? If so, in what way and what do you need to do?**

2. GUIDE YOU INTO ALL TRUTH. The Holy Spirit, who is called "the Spirit of truth" (v. 13), will help us know and understand the truth of God as revealed in creation, the Scriptures, and especially in Christ. As we interact with Scripture, He can direct our study, bring a parallel passage to mind, or lead us to talk to a mentor or teacher. He also helps us recall memorized Scripture when we face decisions, crises, temptation, and ministry opportunities. Someone once told me memorizing Scripture is like increasing the Holy Spirit's vocabulary in your life.

> **How has the Holy Spirit recently guided you in your pursuit of truth? Be specific.**

3. TELL YOU ABOUT THE FUTURE. I often need guidance or assurance as I think about the days, months, and years ahead. The Holy Spirit doesn't speak on His own, but He tells us what He has heard. This doesn't guarantee that the Spirit will provide us with details about future personal events. It does mean He will show what is ahead for those who follow Christ, which He has done through Scripture. And, as we submit to Him, He will faithfully guide us into that future.

What are some things the Holy Spirit has revealed about the future in Scripture that excites you? That frightens you? That challenges you?

4. TELL US WHAT HE RECEIVES FROM JESUS. The Holy Spirit will share with us the words of Jesus. This last promise also speaks to the source and authority by which He shares with us. He's not making things up on His own. Everything comes from Jesus, who has received all things from the Father.

As you consider this work of the Holy Spirit, how are you inspired to interact with Him differently?

If you struggled to answer that question, here is an idea that has proved beneficial in my life. Write these four prayers on a sticky note and put it on your bathroom mirror, the dashboard of your car, or somewhere you will see it throughout the day. Then use these prayer prompts each time you see the sticky for the next three days:

- Holy Spirit, convict me of sin today.

- Holy Spirit, guide me into truth today.

- Holy Spirit, show me what the future holds.

- Holy Spirit, remind me of Jesus's words.

BIRTH

READ JOHN 16:16-22 and circle the letter that best answers the questions according to the text:

What were the disciples confused about (vv. 16-19)?

A. Jesus saying they wouldn't see Him and then they would in a little while.

B. Jesus saying the Holy Spirit would tell them the future.

C. Jesus saying sadness would be turned joy.

Jesus used what example to illustrate grief being turned to joy (v. 21)?

    A.   A butterfly coming from a caterpillar

    B.   The birth of a baby

    C.   The growth of a plant

In these verses, Jesus was trying to prepare His friends for what was about to happen to Him. There would be pain and grief, followed by joy when they saw Him again. I love it that Jesus used a timeless feminine example of childbirth to illustrate life on the other side of labor! As we follow Christ, despite being on this side of the resurrection, we still face days of pain, sorrow, and grief. While His presence and provision carries us through these days, we long for the day when we will see Him again and all will be made right, when our sadness will forever be turned to joy.

How does the promise of His joy-filled return give new perspective to your current challenges?

Jesus lived these truths as He approached the cross, grieving the coming pain but celebrating ultimate salvation.

PRAYER

READ JOHN 16:23-33 and answer the following questions:

Who can you ask directly for your needs (v. 23)?

How does Jesus describe the Father's feelings for believers (v. 27)?

Why can we take heart and have peace in the midst of trials and sorrows (v. 33)?

(Multiple choice answers: A, B)

Jesus emphasized that asking in His name gives us direct access to the Father, a Father who loves us. And that no matter what we go through, we can savor His peace because He has overcome the world.

STOP AND SAVOR

Today we focused on this truth: *Jesus promised peace in the midst of chaos through His Spirit and prayer.*

Summarize your personal takeaway from today's lesson.

What words of Jesus from John 16 do you need the Holy Spirit to remind you of in the coming weeks?

What do you need to ask for in Jesus's name as you think about your current challenges?

Day Five
PRAYER PROMISES

When my children ask me to pray for them, I often add some petitions for what I think they need to what they think they need. Over the years I've prayed for break-ups, consistent spiritual routines, attitude adjustments, and other desires I have for them that weren't on their lists. The consistency and content of my prayers for them expose what I really believe about God.

In John 17, Jesus finished His farewell discourse with a prayer for Himself, His disciples, and all those who believe in Him, including you and me. In this prayer we will discover something vitally important Jesus wants for all of us.

PRAYING FOR HIMSELF

READ JOHN 17:1-5 and label the following statement PR for Prayer Requests or TH for Theology—something we learn about God.

____ Glorify me so I can give glory back to you.

____ The Father has given the Son authority.

____ The Father gives the Son those who will receive eternal life.

____ The way to eternal life is to know the Father and the Son.

____ Bring me into the glory we shared before the world began.

The first and last statements were Jesus's prayers for Himself. The other statements reveal theological truths about the work of Father and Son and provide the definition of *eternal life*—intimate knowledge of God through Christ. By beginning with praying for Himself, Jesus reminds us we can ask for God's goodness to be displayed in our lives, not for our own benefit, but for His glory.

SCRIPTURE FOCUS
John 17

BIG IDEA
We can know what Jesus wants for us through His prayer for us.

John 17 contains the Lord's longest recorded prayer in Scripture and is sometimes referred to as the "high priestly prayer" because of its tone of consecration.[15]

What are you currently praying for yourself and how is it connected to God's goodness being displayed in your life?

I'm asking God to help me complete the work He has given me today. This includes household tasks, answering emails, studying, writing, and resting. I'm praying that in all these things I would be faithful and bring glory to the Lord. Jesus prayed for Himself and we can too.

PRAYING FOR HIS DISCIPLES (vv. 6-19)

The bulk of Jesus's prayer centered on supplications for His disciples.

A name in biblical times authoritatively represented the person it described.[16]

READ JOHN 17:6-19 and list the specific requests Jesus prayed for His disciples in the following verses:

VERSE(S)	JESUS'S SPECIFIC PRAYER REQUESTS
Verse 11	
Verse 15	
Verse 17	

Jesus prayed for the disciples' protection, unity, safety, and holiness. What stands out to you from these petitions?

Despite facing impending betrayal and arrest, Jesus was thinking of His disciples. Since we have His words recorded, we can assume He prayed out loud so they could hear Him. During the season of my father battling cancer, I was prayed for frequently. The women in my Bible study, friends, and my husband talked to the Lord out loud in my presence asking for my comfort, patience, and direction. Knowing that others were lifting up prayers on my behalf reminded me of God's care and attention during that difficult time.

> **What brothers or sisters in Christ need you to pray for them today as Jesus prayed for His friends? Write initials or names next to these requests and take a moment to lift them up in prayer right now.**
>
> **Protection**
>
>
> **Unity**
>
>
> **Safety**
>
>
> **Holiness**
>
>
> **While we learn about prayer from this section of John 17, we also gain greater insight into the character and work of the Father and Son. Based on the verses we just read, label the following truths as describing the Father (F) or Jesus (J).**
>
> _____ **He gave those who belonged to Him to Jesus (vv. 6,10).**
>
> _____ **He gave Jesus His name (v. 11).**
>
> _____ **He told His followers many things so they would be filled with joy (v. 13).**
>
> _____ **He gave the disciples the Father's word (v. 14).**
>
> _____ **He gave Himself as a sacrifice so that His followers could be made holy (v. 19).**

PRAYING FOR US

In the final section of His prayer, Jesus prayed for all believers—that includes you and me!

READ JOHN 17:20-26 and list Jesus's specific prayer requests:

VERSE	JESUS'S SPECIFIC PRAYER REQUESTS
Verse 21	
Verse 22	
Verse 23	
Verse 24	

What main theme stood out to you from Jesus's prayer for us?

Why was our unity so important to Jesus (vv. 21,23)?

Jesus prayed for unity not uniformity. He wasn't praying we would dress the same, act the same, or even agree on every nuance of our faith in cookie cutter fashion. He was praying we would be one in heart and purpose for the gospel, because evidently our unity and love for each other are key components to the effectiveness of our witness (John 13:34-35).

I can't help but feel the tension of Jesus's prayer for unity in a time when Christians seem so divided. We may disagree about baptism, women in ministry, worship styles, and a hundred other things, but we should be able to get on the same page at the foot of the cross and the empty tomb. Let the gospel be our rallying cry! When it comes to non-gospel issues, let's discuss with curiosity, study with diligence, and if needed, disagree with love. And like Jesus, pray for unity!

Let's note one other factor about unity. Go back to John 17:23, and write how much the Father loves those who believe in Jesus.

I'm just reveling in this fact right now. The Father loves us as much as He loves Jesus! The same love the Father loves Jesus with is now on us and in us. Thus, we get to participate in the loving communion with the Father, Son, and Holy Spirit. That is incredible! Seeing other believers (especially those we disagree with) framed in this understanding of how the Father loves all of us should propel us to take steps toward unity.

Who is the Lord calling you to see as a person loved by the Father today? What practical affirmations can you extend to that person this week?

Maybe you want to remind a brother or sister in Christ that God loves them as much as He loves His Son. Or you could text someone a short prayer, write an encouraging note, or say something affirming in front of others. I can't help but smile thinking how these actions will help us be a part of the answer to Jesus's prayer for unity!

STOP AND SAVOR

Today we focused on this truth: *We can know what Jesus wants for us through His prayer for us.*

Summarize your personal takeaway from today's lesson.

What do you savor most from Jesus's prayer?

How does knowing that the Father loves each of us as much as He loves Jesus shape your view of yourself? Of others?

Father, I'm in awe that You love me as much as You love Jesus. Help me to know You better so I can love You more fully. I struggle to be unified with other believers who are different from me. Show me what unity looks like in answer to Jesus's prayer. Thank You for all the precious promises I've discovered this week. Help me to hold onto them when life is hard. In Jesus's name, Amen.

Video Viewer Guide

Because people are _____, disappointment is
_____.

Jesus promised an Advocate to _____ you (John 14:16-17,
26-27; 15:26; 16:13).

Jesus promised to _____ for your _____
(John 17:15,17,20-21,23).

> "Therefore he is able, once and forever, to save those who come
> to God through him. He lives forever to _____ with
> God on their behalf."
>
> HEBREWS 7:25, NLT

> "My dear children, I am writing this to you so that you will not
> sin. But if anyone does sin, we have an _____ who
> pleads our case before the Father. He is Jesus Christ, the one
> who is truly righteous."
>
> 1 JOHN 2:1, NLT

Jesus promised to _____ us spiritually.

We can't do anything _____ Jesus without being _____ Jesus
(John 15:4-5).

CHALLENGE FOR THE WEEK: Identify where you have been
spiritually pulling away—from prayer, from studying God's Word,
from your community of faith. Also take time to determine what is
causing you to distance yourself. Lay all this before the Lord. Repent.
Lean back in to your relationship with Him.

(Answers are available on p. 185.)

GROUP DISCUSSION GUIDE

SHARE: What plant have you kept alive the longest? (You don't have to know the name of it. You can just describe it.)

WATCH the video "Session Six: Savoring Peace in the Promises of Jesus" together and follow along with the viewer guide on the previous page.

MEMORY VERSE: Review John 14:27 and provide time for group members to recite it aloud.

VIDEO DISCUSSION

1. *Ask:* What is it about the person and work of the Holy Spirit in your life that comforts and encourages you the most?

2. *Discuss:* What are some daily practices that help believers stay connected to Jesus?

STUDY DISCUSSION

1. Call on a volunteer to read aloud John 14:1. *Ask:* How does thinking about where you'll go in the next life brighten your outlook today? (p. 125)

2. Discuss the different roles of the Holy Spirit found in Day Two and ask participants which part of John 14 resonates with them most in their current circumstances.

3. Read aloud John 15:1-8. *Ask:* What spiritual truths about your relationship with God emerge from this gardening illustration? (p. 133)

4. Encourage participants to share and discuss their answers to the questions in the Stop and Savor section for Day Four on page 140?

5. *Ask:* What main theme stood out to you from Jesus's prayer for us? (p. 144) Why?

REVIEW the Big Idea for each of the five days of study. Ask for final thoughts or questions regarding the study of God's promises this week.

PRAYER: Allow each woman to share a prayer request. Then instruct each group member to pray silently and lift up the request of the woman on her right.

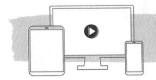

To access the video teaching sessions, use the instructions in the back of your Bible study book.

SESSION
SEVEN

PEACE IN THE
PASSION
OF JESUS

BUT THESE ARE WRITTEN SO THAT

YOU MAY CONTINUE TO BELIEVE

THAT JESUS IS THE MESSIAH,

THE SON OF GOD, AND THAT BY

BELIEVING IN HIM YOU WILL HAVE

LIFE BY THE POWER OF HIS NAME.

John 20:31

Day One

PASSION FOR A GREATER KINGDOM

SCRIPTURE FOCUS

John 18

Today I mailed three bills, called two businesses, drove to a restaurant to retrieve the credit card I left there last night, sorted and filed a stack of mail, stopped by a previous address to pick up a package, and answered three thousand emails. OK, maybe it only felt like three thousand. The stuff of life can feel all-consuming at times.

BIG IDEA

We can spend less time stressing over earthly pursuits when we remember that Jesus's kingdom is not of this world.

What earthly tasks or situations are currently consuming you?

These tasks are often necessary—dishwashers need unloading, diapers need changing, and emails need answering! But here's the danger, if we aren't careful, these earthly concerns can crowd out our passion for God's kingdom.

John wrote the most detailed description of what is referred to as the Passion of Christ—the week of the crucifixion and resurrection of Jesus. It comes from the Latin word *passionem* which means "suffering, enduring."[1]

My prayer is that in studying the passion week, our personal passion will be stirred. We will be moved to lift our eyes from tasks, emails, errands, and all the stuff of life and seek His kingdom first (Matt. 6:33).

VOLUNTEER, NOT VICTIM

READ JOHN 18:1-11 and answer the following questions:

Who accompanied Judas to the garden and what did they have in their possession?

What statement of identity did Jesus make three times in this encounter (vv. 5,6,8)?

What question did Jesus ask after telling Peter to put away his sword?

"The name *Gethsemane* means 'oil press.'" The olives from trees in the garden were pressed into oil, which is "a picture of suffering."[2]

Jesus wasn't a victim of circumstance; He voluntarily surrendered to the hard parts of the Father's call. So far Jesus had eluded capture by the religious authorities. But Judas led them to this secluded spot. They brought weapons believing Jesus might try to slip away again. However, Jesus had nothing to hide. He had been protected from arrest previously because His time had not yet come. Now His time had arrived. He proceeded willingly to drink the cup of suffering.

When considering our own suffering, we don't have to fear, knowing Jesus has gone before us. We are not alone. He is well-acquainted with sorrow (Isa. 53:3) and knows everything we might experience (Heb. 4:15).

"The drinking of a cup is often used in Scripture to illustrate experiencing suffering or sorrow" (Isa. 51:17; Jer. 25:15-28).[3]

> **If you are currently experiencing some challenges, write a few words or phrases describing your difficulties below.**

I'm currently grieving the loss of my father, mourning the poor choices of a wayward child, and missing the close community we left behind in a move. Take a moment to acknowledge the pain in your life, but seek God's help in walking through your suffering. He will be with you to help you change or endure, all for His purpose. Plus, keep in mind, God will transform your current difficulties into glory (2 Cor. 4:17-18).

IMPERFECT LEADERS

READ JOHN 18:15-18,25-27 and write anything that stands out to you about Peter's denial.

We know from Luke's Gospel that Jesus healed the servant Malchus's ear, which was His last recorded miracle before the cross (Luke 22:51).

John set up a contrast for us. When questioned, Jesus said, "I AM" (vv. 5-8). But Peter kept saying, "I am not." Jesus stood up to His questioners and denied nothing. Peter cowered before his questioners and denied everything. Peter fought the wrong enemy with the wrong weapon, slept when he should have been praying, and talked when he should have been listening. Then he denied Jesus three times.

We'll see later that Jesus forgave and restored Peter and eventually lifted him into leadership (John 21). Peter made impulsive decisions, but he turned away from sin and turned back to God. Soon we will find him preaching to multitudes about the gospel of Christ (Acts 2:14-41). Thankfully, Christ's kingdom makes room for imperfect leaders. No matter what we've done in the past, God can use us if we turn from our sin and turn toward Him.

How have you seen God use imperfect leaders (including yourself)?

As we consider Peter, we can exhibit grace for our leaders. They're human, just like us. So they aren't always going to get it right. We can also show grace to ourselves. The enemy wants to drown us in shame, extinguish hope, and convince us to give in to further temptation. Instead, we can confess our sin, turn from it, and experience forgiveness, which inspires change and hope.

GOD'S KINGDOM

READ JOHN 18:12-14,19-24,28-40 and list the people involved in leading Jesus's trials. Note how they are described and the actions they took.

VERSES	PERSON	DESCRIPTION/ACTIONS
Verses 13,24		

VERSES	PERSON	DESCRIPTION/ACTIONS
Verses 14,28		
Verses 29,33-40		

What stood out to you from Jesus's dialogue with those questioning Him?

I couldn't help but notice some huge contrasts between earthly kingdoms and Jesus's greater kingdom.

1. Caiaphas said it would be better for one man to die for the people (John 11:50; 18:14).

   - *Earthly kingdom:* Caiaphas was saying it would be better to kill one man to quell the disturbance than let it go on and the Roman government destroy the nation.

   - *Greater kingdom:* One man, Jesus, died for all, to pay the price for their sins.

2. Jesus's accusers didn't want to go inside the headquarters of the Roman government because they didn't want to defile themselves before Passover (18:28).

   - *Earthly kingdom:* Jews took precautions to avoid contamination in order to eat the Passover while at the same time manipulating the judicial system to kill an innocent man.

   - *Greater kingdom:* Jesus is the ultimate Passover Lamb who takes away the sin of the world.

3. The people asked for the criminal Barabbas to be released rather than Jesus (18:38-40).

   - *Earthly kingdom:* Barabbas's name means "son of a father."[4]

   - *Greater kingdom:* Jesus is the Son of the Father.

Individuals concerned with earthly kingdoms stressed over temporary problems. Jesus's greater kingdom was concerned with eternal restoration. Jesus taught about a reverse economy that values service, humility, forgiveness and love.

Let's take a moment to check our own hearts. Where have earthly concerns overshadowed Jesus's kingdom priorities in your life lately?

Peter showed us that no matter how far we've gotten off track, we can be restored and walk in a new direction.

STOP AND SAVOR

Today we focused on this truth: *We can spend less time stressing over earthly pursuits when we remember that Jesus's kingdom is not of this world.*

Summarize your personal takeaway from today's lesson?

What words of Jesus stood out to you today?

How does Peter's restoration encourage you?

Day Two
A PASSIONATE PRICE

Now that my children are grown, I look back and wish I'd been more present and patient when they were little. You may not have mom guilt, but I imagine you have some stories you would rewrite. Maybe you would be less angry, set better boundaries, or establish better habits. We have an enemy who loves to remind us of past sins and failures in hopes that guilt would drive us to despair.

As we read the account of Jesus's death on the cross, we don't want to merely feel sad for what He suffered. We don't just contemplate the cross—we carry it with us, savoring these gospel truths and believing that His death brings us life today and every day. Everything you feel guilty about today was wiped out two thousand years ago on the cross!

Today, we will connect Old Testament prophecy with its New Testament fulfillment to see that Jesus offered Himself as the perfect Passover Lamb to remove our guilt.

SCRIPTURE FOCUS
John 19

BIG IDEA
Jesus offered Himself as the perfect Passover Lamb to remove our guilt.

THE SILENT LAMB

READ JOHN 19:1-16 and answer the following questions:

How was Jesus treated (vv. 1-3)?

What did the Jewish leaders state as Jesus's offense (v. 7)?

What emotion did Pilate express when he heard the charge against Jesus (v. 8)?

The crown of thorns was possibly made "from the branches of the thorny acanthus shrub or from the date palm."[5]

Summarize what Jesus said when He finally spoke to Pilate (v. 11).

Jesus didn't answer Pilate's questions or defend Himself. He fulfilled prophecy with His silence.

> He was oppressed and treated harshly, yet he never said a word. He was led like a lamb to the slaughter. And as a sheep is silent before the shearers, he did not open his mouth.
> ISAIAH 53:7

When we consider the severity of the beating Jesus took, His silence in the face of such grave injustice feels even more compelling. Roman soldiers used a whip made of leather thongs with pieces of bone or metal attached, and typically only stopped from their own exhaustion or when an officer in authority commanded it.[6]

As I reflect on this passage, I'm moved knowing that what Jesus endured was meant for me. He carried it for me, for us. I'm also struck by Jesus's firm trust in God's sovereignty even as He was mocked and beaten. It reminds us that no power can touch us except what is allowed from above.

What stands out to you after reading these verses?

THE ROYAL LAMB

READ JOHN 19:17-27 and then read the following Old Testament prophecies. Write the verse number in John that fulfills each prophecy:

VERSE IN JOHN 19	OLD TESTAMENT PROPHECY
	I will give him the honors of a victorious soldier, because he exposed himself to death. He was counted among the rebels. He bore the sins of many and interceded for rebels. *Isaiah 53:12*

VERSE IN JOHN 19	OLD TESTAMENT PROPHECY
	They divide my garments among themselves and throw dice for my clothing. *Psalm 22:18*

Historical descriptions of the crucifixion vary slightly. One scholar describes Jesus laying down on the cross where His arms and legs were nailed and then hoisted up a piece of wood that served as a kind of seat which partially supported His weight. This wasn't designed to relieve agony but to increase it.[7] "To breathe, it was necessary to push with the legs and pull with the arms to keep the chest cavity open and functioning. Terrible muscle spasm wracked the entire body; but since collapse meant asphyxiation, the strain went on and on."[8]

In the midst of this terrible agony, Jesus spoke tenderly to His mother. Likely four women stood watching: Jesus's mother, her sister, Mary the wife of Clopas, and Mary Magdalene.[9] Jesus wanted to be sure His mother was cared for and assigned John, the writer of the Gospel, to meet her needs.

In the Roman world of Jesus's day, the language they spoke was Aramaic, the official language of the empire was Latin, and the language common for written communication was Greek.[10]

THE FINAL LAMB

READ JOHN 19:28-37 and again write the verse number(s) corresponding with fulfilled prophecy:

VERSE IN JOHN 19	OLD TESTAMENT PROPHECY
	But instead, they give me poison for food; they offer me sour wine for my thirst. *Psalm 69:21*
	For the LORD protects the bones of the righteous; not one of them is broken! *Psalm 34:20* Each Passover lamb must be eaten in one house. Do not carry any of its meat outside, and do not break any of its bones. *Exodus 12:46*
	Then I will pour out a spirit of grace and prayer on the family of David and on the people of Jerusalem. They will look on me whom they have pierced and mourn for him as for an only son. They will grieve bitterly for him as for a firstborn son who has died. *Zechariah 12:10*

The sour wine Jesus asked for fulfilled prophecy and was also meant to moisten Jesus's lips so He could speak loudly enough for the crowd to hear His final words.[12]

After drinking the cup of suffering, Jesus cried out *tetelestai*, a Greek expression that means, "it is finished." This was no cry of defeat or announcement of impending death. *Tetelestai* was an expression used in everyday life: a servant letting a master know he had finished a task, an artist or writer finishing a project, a merchant declaring a debt was paid in full, or a priest declaring an animal sacrifice faultless.[11]

Jesus had completed all the Father asked of Him.

Jesus was the perfect Lamb of God whom John the Baptist identified early in John's Gospel:

> The next day John saw Jesus coming toward him and said, "Look! The Lamb of God who takes away the sin of the world! He is the one I was talking about when I said, 'A man is coming after me who is far greater than I am, for he existed long before me.'"
> JOHN 1:29-30

Jesus's death declared our sin debt is paid in full. We can live without guilt because Jesus purchased our forgiveness through His shed blood.

How does reading the details of Jesus's sacrifice bring fresh appreciation for the passionate price of your forgiveness?

As I consider that question, I feel grateful. I can savor peace today because Jesus endured the cross for me. I may still feel conviction when I sin, but the weight of guilt is gone.

BURIAL OF THE LAMB

READ JOHN 19:38-42 and identify the two men who were responsible for Jesus's burial.

1.

2.

We know little about Joseph of Arimathea apart from his involvement in securing permission and a place for Christ's burial. John is the only gospel writer who includes the detail about Nicodemus's participation. As men familiar with the law, both Joseph and Nicodemus likely recognized the prophecy we've explored today and believed that Jesus fulfilled the Passover as the slain Lamb of God.

His shed blood covers us from the penalty of sin. We have life through His sacrifice. While we don't savor that Jesus suffered, we can savor all that His suffering accomplished.

STOP AND SAVOR

Today we focused on this truth: *Jesus offered Himself as the perfect Passover Lamb to remove our guilt.*

Summarize your personal takeaway from today's lesson.

The seventy-five pounds of spices were worth a hundred years' wages. "The extravagance underlines the devotion of these formerly secret believers."[13]

How does this story, which is anything but peaceful, bring us peace?

PRAYER

Jesus, thank You for willingly enduring the cross for me. I'm so grateful that I don't have to live with guilt and shame. Help me to remember the passionate price You paid to remove my guilt and secure my peace with God. You are the Messiah, the Lamb of God who takes away my sin! In Jesus's name, Amen.

What guilt do you need to leave at the foot of the cross today?

Day Three

PASSIONATE PEACE

I remember sitting on a bus in middle school, staring out the window and reasoning with God about His existence. My twelve-year-old brain wondered if I would have believed in a different religion if I'd been born in another region of the world. I asked God to help me know if He was truly the real God of the universe. It was the reasoning of a preteen wanting to know if God was real and worth spending my life following.

Since then, I have studied God's Word and many belief systems of other faiths. One event has deepened my faith like nothing else. If John's Gospel had ended at chapter 19, Jesus would have been an exceptional character who made extraordinary claims. What sets Jesus apart from every other religious or moral teacher is His empty tomb.

The apostle Paul wrote a letter to the church at Corinth referencing the resurrection this way: "And if Christ has not been raised, then all our preaching is useless, and your faith is useless" (1 Cor. 15:14). As we read John 20 today, I pray we will move toward greater faith as we review the first followers' responses to the empty tomb.

PETER AND JOHN RUNNING

READ JOHN 20:1-10 and order the following events, 1 to 6.

_____ Peter arrived at the tomb and immediately went in.

_____ Mary found the stone rolled away from the tomb.

_____ Peter and the beloved disciple both ran to the tomb.

_____ The beloved disciple entered the tomb and believed that Jesus rose from the dead.

_____ Mary ran and told two disciples that Jesus's body was not in the tomb.

_____ The beloved disciple outran Peter but did not go into the tomb.

BIG IDEA
We can move toward greater faith as we review the first followers' responses to the empty tomb.

As a reminder, who is the beloved disciple?

Remember that John never referred to himself by name in his Gospel—always "the one whom Jesus loved." It cracks me up that he included his victory over Peter in the footrace to the tomb (v. 4). Throughout John's Gospel, Jesus's pace had been slow and deliberate. Now the disciples were running, motivated by powerful emotions as they processed Jesus's death.

Can you think of a time when maybe you weren't physically running to investigate the claims of Jesus but perhaps you were running mentally, academically, or emotionally toward Him? If so, write a short description of your forward motion.

We know from the other Gospel accounts that multiple women were going to the tomb along with Mary to finish anointing Jesus with spices.[14]

MARY CRYING

READ JOHN 20:11-18. **What convinced Mary the man she was speaking to was Jesus?**

Jesus first appeared in bodily form to a crying woman. When Mary heard her name, she knew it was the Lord. She likely prostrated herself at Jesus's feet and held onto Him (Matt. 28:9). Jesus then sent her to declare His appearance to His "brothers" (John 20:17) referring to His disciples. When Jesus mentioned "my Father and your Father, to my God and your God," He was including Mary in the kingdom family with His language.[15]

Jesus rose for Mary, and for you and me. Believing in Him brings us into the same kingdom family. Whether this week has included running toward Jesus or crying in confusion, we can rest our faith on the fact that Jesus is alive!

THE DISCIPLES FEARING

READ JOHN 20:19-23 **and write the repeated phrase Jesus spoke to His disciples in verses 19 and 21.**

In the culture of Jesus's day, a woman's testimony was not valued or seen as credible. That validates John's reporting that Jesus first appeared to a woman, Mary Magdalene. It also shows how Jesus's values were far different from His culture.[16]

The disciples met in a room with locked doors because they feared the Jewish leaders. After He repeated the peace greeting, He then:

- Sent them out as the Father had sent Him. They were not to stay huddled up behind closed doors but to go into all the world with the gospel.

- Breathed on them to receive the Holy Spirit. Scholars debate what this means in light of Acts 2. Some say it was a temporary filling while others say it was a spiritual endowment, preparing them for what would take place at Pentecost.[17]

- Highlighted that forgiveness was at the center of their message. They wouldn't have power and authority to forgive, but they would have the power and authority to proclaim forgiveness found in Christ.[18]

Jesus commissioned the disciples in the midst of their fears. We face our own brand of fear. Maybe our finances, health, or relationships have us locking the doors of our hearts. But Jesus speaks peace over us in the midst of troubling circumstances and sends us out in the power of the Holy Spirit with the message of forgiveness. We don't need to wait until we're fear-free to follow Jesus.

How has the peace of Jesus freed you to serve and share even in the midst of your current challenges?

THOMAS DOUBTING

READ JOHN 20:24-29 and describe in your own words Jesus's response to Thomas.

Clearly Thomas hadn't totally abandoned his faith because he continued to meet with the disciples. Jesus knew Thomas's struggle and didn't shame him. Instead, Jesus provided what Thomas needed to move from doubt to faith.

This encounter reminds us that we can press into our doubts with Christ, exploring, asking questions, and genuinely seeking truth.

How does Thomas's experience encourage you when it comes to doubts, whether your own or those experienced by people in your circle of influence?

Have you ever wondered what it means to be great? If so, check out the digging deeper article titled, "Defining Greatness" found online at lifeway.com/gospelofjohn.

YOU AND I BELIEVING

READ JOHN 20:30-31 and fill in the blanks below:

"But these are written so that you may continue to _____ that Jesus is the Messiah, the Son of God, and that by believing in him you will have _____ by the power of his name" (John 20:31, NLT).

John made clear his purpose in recording this account of Jesus's life, death, and resurrection—so we might believe in Him and have life in His name. Hallelujah!

STOP AND SAVOR

Today we focused on this truth: *We can move toward greater faith as we review the first followers' responses to the empty tomb.*

Summarize your personal takeaway from today's lesson.

What words and actions of Jesus are you particularly savoring from John 20? Why?

How has Jesus met you personally in your confusion, fear, heartbreak, or doubt?

PRAYER

Jesus, I know You are the Son of God. You died, but You rose from the dead. When I run, help me to run toward You. When I'm sad, help me to bring my sadness to You. When I'm afraid, help me to find peace in You. When I'm doubting, helping me to work through my questions with You. Fill me with Your Holy Spirit so I can proclaim the gospel and serve others in Your love. In Jesus's name, Amen.

Day Four

PASSION FOR PEOPLE

SCRIPTURE FOCUS
John 21:1-24

BIG IDEA
Vertical love for Jesus propels us toward horizontal care for others.

Social media helps me keep up with old friends, hear inspiration from Bible teachers, and laugh at amusing videos. However, I can also get sidetracked by advertised products or find myself coveting other peoples' vacations, accomplishments, or seemingly uncomplicated lives. Sometimes looking sideways at others' lives prevents me from looking up at Jesus.

In what ways do you find yourself similarly distracted?

I will sometimes open my phone to text someone, but because I first check Facebook® and email, I forget why I even picked up my phone! When it comes to our love for Jesus, we want to stay focused knowing that vertical love for Jesus propels us toward horizontal care for others.

FUTILE FISHING

On the Sea of Galilee, nighttime is reported to be the time for more productive fishing. The catch could then be brought in and sold in the morning.[19]

READ JOHN 21:1-3 and answer the following questions:

Why do you think they decided to go fishing?

How long did they fish and what did they catch?

The disciples knew Jesus was alive and had promised them His Spirit. They waited at the Sea of Galilee (also called the Sea of Tiberius) likely because Jesus told them He would meet them in Galilee (Matt. 28:7; Mark 16:7). Peter announced that he was going fishing and the others followed his lead. His motivation to head out to sea is not given in the text. Maybe he got restless. I can relate. Often, we revert to familiar routines when we lack direction. Sitting tight is difficult. But when we move without divine inspiration, we often end up with only perspiration to show for it.

When have you struggled to know what came next in God's plan? How did you deal with being unsure where to go or what to do?

If you're currently in one of those seasons, how are you doing with sitting tight?

The disciples didn't have to wait long. Jesus showed up with encouragement and direction. In His time, He will provide clarity for you, too!

FAITH FISHING

READ JOHN 21:4-14 and draw a line from the person to the action or statement. (Some people will be used more than once.)

He told the disciples to throw their nets on the right side of the boat.

He said, "It is the Lord!"

Jesus

He put on his tunic and jumped in the water.

Peter

He dragged the fish-filled net to shore.

John, the beloved disciple

He invited the disciples to eat breakfast.

When Jesus directed their fishing, the disciples pulled in "153 large fish" (v. 11). It's pure speculation to see any significance to the number. John probably included the detail because it was such a large amount. What we can know from this number is that things get exciting when Jesus shows up! When we follow His instructions by faith, we can accomplish exponentially more than what is humanly possible.

Have you ever experienced a spiritual breakthrough after hours of your own self effort? If so, explain.

Seasons of waiting can cause us to overfocus on natural methods to discern God's direction, like pros and cons lists, spreadsheets, or Google® searches. These aren't necessarily harmful practices as long as we are looking up more than sideways for guidance.

SHEPHERDING SHEEP

READ JOHN 21:15-17 and fill in the chart with the missing information. (Answers will vary depending on translation.)

VERSE	JESUS'S QUESTION	PETER'S ANSWER	JESUS'S RESPONSE
Verse 15	Do you love me more than these?		Feed my lambs.
Verse 16		Yes, Lord. You know I love you.	Take care of my sheep.
Verse 17	Do you love me?		

Two different Greek words for "love" are used in this passage: *agapao*—divine love (Jesus's first two questions) and *phileo*—brotherly love (Jesus's third question and Peter's three replies).[20] However, the consensus among commentators is that we shouldn't read too much into the word variance, especially since the original conversation likely took place in Aramaic.[21] John's Greek word choice likely had more to do with his writing style than disclosing a hidden meaning about types of love.[22]

Peter had previously made some pretty bold boasts. He said:

- He would die for Jesus (John 13:37).

- He would never desert Jesus, even if everyone else did (Matt. 26:33).

- He would never disown or deny Jesus, even if it cost his life (Matt. 26:35).

But in this moment, instead of bragging, Peter was broken. He had grossly overestimated his abilities. I can't help but put myself in Peter's shoes.

How have you experienced humility on the other side of failure?

I'm feeling it today. Yesterday I blew off my healthy eating plan, shirked work responsibilities, and was irritable with my husband. I woke up discouraged at 4:00 a.m. and couldn't get back to sleep. I slipped out of bed and began journaling. I told the Lord everything He already knew and experienced His grace once again. Today I feel especially grateful for Peter's commissioning to feed God's sheep. The Lord doesn't write us off when we fail. He will continue to call us and use us when we turn back to Him in faith.

CARING INSTEAD OF COMPARING

READ JOHN 21:18-24 and write Peter's question in verse 21.

According to church tradition, Peter was crucified upside down, probably in Rome during the reign of emperor Nero.[23]

Have you been asking some version of that question as you compare your situation to others? You don't have to write anything; just consider whether you're distracted from keeping your eyes up toward God because you've been focused sideways on those around you.

Maybe you wish you had her health, his job, their ministry, or something else. When Jesus told Peter that imprisonment and death lay ahead for him, Peter turned around and asked about John. Jesus redirected Peter to leave other peoples' callings to Him. This truth is easier to read, study, and discuss than to live out.

Where is the Lord challenging you to keep your eyes on Him and away from comparative living?

What practices help you to fix your eyes on Christ?

PRAYER

Jesus, help me to wait for Your directions rather than spinning my wheels in futility. Thank You for showing up with abundance and guiding my efforts. Lord, thank You for restoring Peter. His story reminds me that You are restoring me on the other side of my failures. Help me to keep my eyes fixed on You so I can care for those around me without comparing. In Jesus's name, Amen.

Rather than measure the trials and blessings of others, we must keep our eyes on Jesus and seek God's glory in His call for us.

STOP AND SAVOR

Today we focused on this truth: *Vertical love for Jesus propels us toward horizontal care for others.*

Summarize your personal takeaway from today's lesson.

Jesus blessed His disciples with food and fellowship after He rose from the dead. What blessings from Jesus can you identify in your life today?

How does Jesus's interaction with Peter help you savor His peace?

Day Five

MORE PASSION

As I reflect on my own journey through John, I recognize God's kindness toward me. He knew I would be walking through my dad's cancer and death during this season. Savoring the peace of Jesus in a chaotic world has been a gracious gift in my life during this time.

> **How have you experienced God's kindness during your study of John?**

Today we finish this Gospel and reflect on the impact of Jesus's message in our lives.

PEACE BEYOND OUR UNDERSTANDING

READ JOHN 21:25 and summarize the final verse.

John reminded us that Jesus's ministry could not be captured in one volume, four Gospel accounts, or any number of books. He is the Logos, the Living Word, whose love for His Father and His creation runs deeper than we can wrap our minds or words around. In his letter to the church at Philippi, the apostle Paul confirmed that we can't fully grasp the extent of what God has given us in Christ:

> Then you will experience God's peace, which exceeds
> anything we can understand. His peace will guard
> your hearts and minds as you live in Christ Jesus.
> **PHILIPPIANS 4:7**

The gospel of Jesus can't be explained nor contained in any one book, and the peace of Jesus also exceeds our understanding! Both overdeliver because of God's kindness toward us.

SCRIPTURE FOCUS
John 21:25

BIG IDEA
We can savor the peace of Jesus in a chaotic world.

PEACE IN THE CHAOS

What challenging situations have you experienced since beginning this study of John's Gospel?

How has God used this study to speak into those situations?

Jesus assured us that in this world, we would have trouble (John 16:33). He tabernacled among us in human form so He felt that trouble personally (1:14). He cried when Lazarus died (11:35). He got angry over abuses in the temple (2:15). He grew weary (4:6). He saw the chaos we experience firsthand. Yet He reminded us that trouble doesn't get the final word.

READ AGAIN these words of Jesus and put a star next to the verses that stand out to you today.

> For this is how God loved the world: He gave his one and only Son, so that everyone who believes in him will not perish but have eternal life.
> JOHN 3:16

> The thief's purpose is to steal and kill and destroy.
> My purpose is to give them a rich and satisfying life.
> JOHN 10:10

> Don't let your hearts be troubled. Trust in God, and trust also in me.
> JOHN 14:1

> I am leaving you with a gift—peace of mind and heart. And the peace I give is a gift the world cannot give. So don't be troubled or afraid.
> JOHN 14:27

> I have told you all this so that you may have peace in me. Here on earth you will have many trials and sorrows. But take heart, because I have overcome the world.
> JOHN 16:33

When Jesus appeared to His disciples after the resurrection, He approached them with the words, "Peace be with you" (John 20:19,21). He speaks peace to us as well. He's not offering the absence of conflict, but a tranquil state of the soul.

PEACE IS A PERSON

We may be turning the last page in John's Gospel, but we don't want to close the book on peace. Peace is a Person, and His name is Jesus. Let's reflect on what John revealed about Him.

Check out the following names and descriptions of Jesus that are found in John's Gospel. Circle a few you have savored during this study:

Water-Walker	True Vine	Logos, Living Word
Way, Truth, Life	Living Water	Creator
Lamb of God	Bread of Life	Healer
Messiah	Son of God	Son of Man
Generous Host	Noticer	Rabbi (Teacher)
Patient	Peace	Light of the World
The Door	Resurrection and Life	

If something from the study stood out to you about Jesus that isn't listed above, write it below.

THE INVITATION TO PEACE

When we lack peace, we lack Jesus. We can answer His invitation to come to Him.

- He told His disciples to "come and see" (John 1:39).

- He stood up at the Feast of Tabernacles asking people to "come and drink" (7:37).

- He appeared after His death with a request to "come and have some breakfast" (21:12).[24]

What was the repeated word in all those sentences?

In what ways are you planning to spend time with Jesus in the coming weeks and months without the structure of this study in John?

We saw in the study that Jesus met with groups of people (John 6; 20:19-23) but also engaged in private conversations (3:2; 4:4-26). We need to meet Him in both. And we need to meet Him regardless of our circumstances. I pray your relationship with Christ will grow as you come to Him in the midst of the celebrations and challenges.

WRAP-UP

Before we end our time together, let's briefly identify takeaways from each session of our study.

Take some time to thoughtfully review what you've learned over the course of the study and record a brief answer to each reflection question.

The seven signs Jesus performed in John include water to wine, healing an official's son, healing a man by the pool, feeding of the five thousand, walking on water, healing a man born blind, and raising Lazarus.

SESSION TITLE	REFLECT	RESPONSE
Peace in the Plan of Jesus John 1–3	As you consider God's unfailing plan to save His people, what plans can you surrender to Him today?	
Peace in the Power of Jesus John 4–6	As you reflect on the seven signs John highlighted, what are you boldly asking God to do in your life? (See margin to review signs.)	
Peace in the Patience of Jesus John 7–9	Where is the Lord calling you to look beneath the surface so you can judge correctly in a current situation?	

SESSION TITLE	REFLECT	RESPONSE
Peace in the Purposes of Jesus John 10–13	How have you experienced God's abundance in a specific way over the course of our time together?	
Peace in the Promises of Jesus John 14–17	How has the Holy Spirit been your Advocate, defending, comforting, and strengthening you?	
Peace in the Passion of Jesus John 18–21	Jesus's passion for you took Him all the way to the cross. Spend a few moments thanking Him for His love.	

Which week of study resonated most personally with you? Why that week?

Thank you for journeying with me through the pages of John. I pray that God's peace will continue to exceed our comprehension in the weeks and months ahead as we savor Jesus above all else in this chaotic world.

STOP AND SAVOR

Today we focused on this truth: *We can savor the peace of Jesus in a chaotic world.*

> **Summarize one or two personal takeaways from this study as a whole.**

Video Viewer Guide

Jesus moves _____ us even when we've moved _____
from Him.

As He did with Mary, Jesus moves those in distress from
_____ to _____ (John 20:1-2,11-18).

As He did with Thomas, Jesus helps doubters _____
(John 20:24-29).

As He did with Peter, Jesus entrusts deniers with His _____
(John 18:15-17; 21:15-17).

> "At that moment the Lord turned and looked at Peter. Suddenly,
> the Lord's words flashed through Peter's mind: 'Before the rooster
> crows tomorrow morning, you will deny three times that you even
> know me.' And Peter left the courtyard, weeping bitterly."

LUKE 22:61-62, NLT

No matter how many times you give God reasons to leave,
He _____.

CHALLENGE FOR THE WEEK: Build the practice, nurture the
discipline of savoring peace in your chaotic world.

(Answers are available on p. 185.)

GROUP DISCUSSION GUIDE

SHARE: When was the last time you went fishing? What was that experience like? If you've never been fishing, what are the sights, sounds, and smells you imagine come along with it?

WATCH the video "Session Seven: Savoring Peace in the Passion of Jesus" together and follow along with the viewer guide on the previous page.

MEMORY VERSE: Review John 20:31 and provide time for group members to recite it aloud.

VIDEO DISCUSSION

1. *Ask:* Which person—Mary, Thomas, or Peter—do you most relate to in this current season of your life? Explain.

2. *Discuss:* What are some practical ways to maintain the habit of stopping and savoring Jesus after this study is over?

STUDY DISCUSSION

1. Discuss the contrast between an earthly kingdom and Jesus's greater kingdom. (p. 153) *Ask:* What earthly tasks or situations are currently consuming you? (p. 150)

2. Call on a volunteer to read John 19:28-37. *Ask:* How does reading the details of Jesus's sacrifice bring fresh appreciation for the passionate price of your forgiveness? (p. 158)

3. Encourage participants to share and discuss their answers to the questions in the Stop and Savor section for Day Three on page 163?

4. *Ask:* Where is the Lord challenging you to keep your eyes on Him and away from comparative living? What practices help you to fix your eyes on Christ? (p. 168)

5. Direct each participant to identify one or two key takeaways from their study of the Gospel of John.

REVIEW the Big Idea for each of the five days of study. Ask for final thoughts or questions regarding the study of God's passion this week.

PRAYER: Ask your group to share prayer requests. Then invite a woman who is comfortable praying out loud to open the prayer time. Give time for others to pray as they feel led to close the session.

To access the video teaching sessions, use the instructions in the back of your Bible study book.

Timeline
FOR THE GOSPEL OF JOHN

26–36
Pontius Pilate is prefect of Judea

AD 18–29

18–36
Caiaphas is high priest

Winter 32/33
Growing opposition to Jesus at the Festival of Dedication

32
Jesus's feeding of the five thousand during Passover

Autumn 32
Jesus's teachings at the Festival of Shelters

Winter 33
Jesus raises Lazarus from the dead

Sunday, Nisan 9, 33
Jesus's triumphal entry into Jerusalem

AD 33

Late Winter 33
Jesus's last journey to Jerusalem via Samaria and Galilee

Monday, Nisan 10, 33
Jesus's second cleansing of the temple

For a more detailed possible timeline of the Gospel of John, check out this website:
https://biblicalfoundations.org/johannine-chronology/

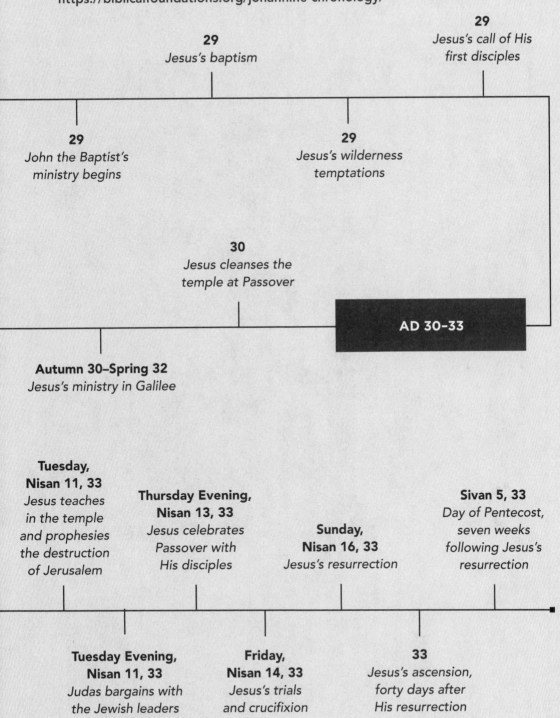

29
Jesus's baptism

29
Jesus's call of His first disciples

29
John the Baptist's ministry begins

29
Jesus's wilderness temptations

30
Jesus cleanses the temple at Passover

AD 30–33

Autumn 30–Spring 32
Jesus's ministry in Galilee

Tuesday, Nisan 11, 33
Jesus teaches in the temple and prophesies the destruction of Jerusalem

Thursday Evening, Nisan 13, 33
Jesus celebrates Passover with His disciples

Sunday, Nisan 16, 33
Jesus's resurrection

Sivan 5, 33
Day of Pentecost, seven weeks following Jesus's resurrection

Tuesday Evening, Nisan 11, 33
Judas bargains with the Jewish leaders to betray Jesus

Friday, Nisan 14, 33
Jesus's trials and crucifixion

33
Jesus's ascension, forty days after His resurrection

Maps
DURING THE TIME OF JOHN

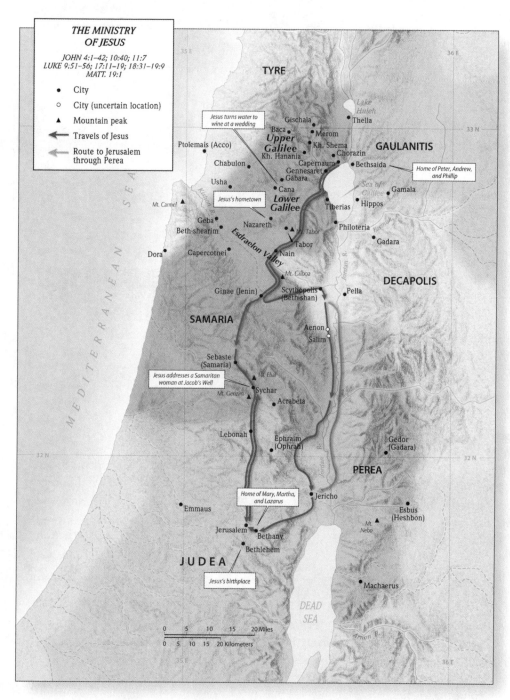

THE MINISTRY OF JESUS

JOHN 4:1–42; 10:40; 11:7
LUKE 9:51–56; 17:11–19; 18:31–19:9
MATT. 19:1

- • City
- ○ City (uncertain location)
- ▲ Mountain peak
- → Travels of Jesus
- → Route to Jerusalem through Perea

TYRE

Jesus turns water to wine at a wedding

Lake Huleh
Gischala
Baca
Merom
Thella
Kh. Shema
Upper Galilee
GAULANITIS
Ptolemais (Acco)
Kh. Hanania
Chorazin
Chabulon
Capernaum
Bethsaida
Home of Peter, Andrew, and Phillip
Gennesaret
Usha
Gabara
Sea of Galilee
Gamala
Cana
Lower Galilee
Tiberias
Hippos
Mt. Carmel
Geba
Nazareth
Mt. Tabor
Philoteria
Beth-shearim
Tabor
Gadara
Dora
Capercotnei
Esdraelon Valley
Nain
Mt. Gilboa
Ginae (Jenin)
Scythopolis (Beth-shan)
Pella
DECAPOLIS

SAMARIA
Aenon
Salim
Sebaste (Samaria)
Mt. Ebal
Jesus addresses a Samaritan woman at Jacob's Well
Mt. Gerizim
Sychar
Acrabeta
Lebonah
Ephraim (Ophrah)
Gedor (Gadara)
PEREA
Home of Mary, Martha, and Lazarus
Jericho
Emmaus
Esbus (Heshbon)
Mt. Nebo
Jerusalem
Bethany
Bethlehem
JUDEA
Jesus's birthplace
Machaerus
DEAD SEA

MEDITERRANEAN SEA

0 5 10 15 20 Miles
0 5 10 15 20 Kilometers

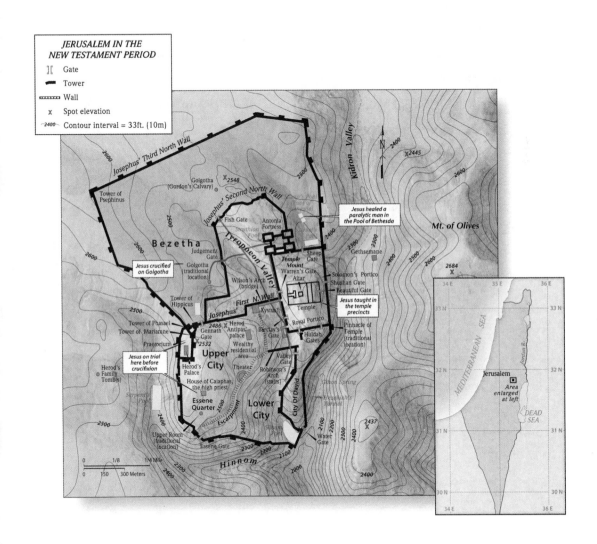

JERUSALEM IN THE NEW TESTAMENT PERIOD

][Gate

🔲 Tower

⚏⚏⚏ Wall

x Spot elevation

-2400- Contour interval = 33ft. (10m)

Josephus' Third North Wall

Tower of Psephinus

Golgotha (Gordon's Calvary)

X 2548

Josephus' Second North Wall

Fish Gate

Antonia Fortress

Jesus healed a paralytic man in the Pool of Bethesda

Mt. of Olives

Kidron Valley

X 2445

Tyropoeon Valley

Bezetha

Judgement Gate

Jesus crucified on Golgotha

Golgotha (traditional location)

Wilson's Arch (bridge)

Temple Mount

Warren's Gate Altar

Sheep Gate

Gethsemane

Solomon's Portico

Shushan Gate

Beautiful Gate

Jesus taught in the temple precincts

X 2684

Tower of Hippicus

First N. Wall

Josephus'

Xystus?

Temple

Tower of Phasael

Tower of Mariamne

Praetorium

2486 X

Gennath Gate

2532

Herod Antipas' palace

Barclay's Gate

Wealthy residential area

Royal Portico

Huldah Gates

Pinnacle of Temple (traditional location)

Jesus on trial here before crucifixion

Herod's Palace

Upper City

Theater

Valley Gate

Robinson's Arch (stairs)

Gihon Spring

2437 X

Herod's Family Tomb(s)

House of Caiaphas, the high priest

Lower City

City Of David

Hezekiah's Tunnel

Serpents Pool

Essene Quarter

Escarpment

Upper Room (traditional location)

Essene Gate

Water Gate

Hinnom

0   1/8   1/4 Mile
0   150   300 Meters

Inset map (Area enlarged at left)

MEDITERRANEAN SEA

Jerusalem
Area enlarged at left

DEAD SEA

Jordan R.

34 E   35 E   36 E

33 N   32 N   31 N   30 N

READ THROUGH JOHN

SESSION TWO: PEACE IN THE PLAN OF JESUS

☐ Day One: John 1:1-34

☐ Day Two: John 1:35-51

☐ Day Three: John 2:1-22

☐ Day Four: John 2:23–3:21

☐ Day Five: John 3:22-36

SESSION THREE: PEACE IN THE POWER OF JESUS

☐ Day One: John 4:1-42

☐ Day Two: John 4:43–5:15

☐ Day Three: John 5:16-45

☐ Day Four: John 6:1-21

☐ Day Five: John 6:22-71

SESSION FOUR: PEACE IN THE PATIENCE OF JESUS

☐ Day One: John 7:1-36

☐ Day Two: John 7:37-52

☐ Day Three: John 8:1-11

☐ Day Four: John 8:12-59

☐ Day Five: John 9

SESSION FIVE: PEACE IN THE PURPOSES OF JESUS

☐ Day One: John 10

☐ Day Two: John 11

☐ Day Three: John 12

☐ Day Four: John 13:1-17

☐ Day Five: John 13:18-35

SESSION SIX: PEACE IN THE PROMISES OF JESUS

☐ Day One: John 14:1-14

☐ Day Two: John 14:15-31

☐ Day Three: John 15

☐ Day Four: John 16

☐ Day Five: John 17

SESSION SEVEN: PEACE IN THE PASSION OF JESUS

☐ Day One: John 18

☐ Day Two: John 19

☐ Day Three: John 20

☐ Day Four: John 21:1-24

☐ Day Five: John 21:25

HOW TO BECOME A CHRISTIAN

Romans 10:17 says, "So faith comes from what is heard, and what is heard comes through the message about Christ."

Maybe you've stumbled across new information in this study. Or maybe you've attended church all your life, but something you read here struck you differently than it ever has before. If you have never accepted Christ but would like to, read on to discover how you can become a Christian.

Your heart tends to run from God and rebel against Him. The Bible calls this sin. Romans 3:23 says, "For everyone has sinned; we all fall short of God's glorious standard."

Yet God loves you and wants to save you from sin, to offer you a new life of hope. John 10:10b says, "My purpose is to give them a rich and satisfying life."

To give you this gift of salvation, God made a way through His Son, Jesus Christ. Romans 5:8 says, "But God showed his great love for us by sending Christ to die for us while we were still sinners."

You receive this gift by faith alone. Ephesians 2:8-9 says, "God saved you by his grace when you believed. And you can't take credit for this; it is a gift from God. Salvation is not a reward for the good things we have done, so none of us can boast about it."

Faith is a decision of your heart demonstrated by the actions of your life. Romans 10:9 says, "If you openly declare that Jesus is Lord and believe in your heart that God raised him from the dead, you will be saved."

If you trust that Jesus died for your sins and want to receive new life through Him, pray a prayer similar to the following to express your repentance and faith in Him:

Dear God, I know I am a sinner. I believe Jesus died to forgive me of my sins. I accept Your offer of eternal life. Thank You for forgiving me of all my sins. Thank You for my new life. From this day forward, I will choose to follow You.

If you have trusted Jesus for salvation, please share your decision with your group leader or another Christian friend. If you are not already attending church, find one in which you can worship and grow in your faith. Following Christ's example, ask to be baptized as a public expression of your faith.

ENDNOTES

Session One

1. *"Eirene,"* Bible Study Tools, accessed Sept. 8, 2023. Available at www.biblestudytools.com/lexicons/greek/nas/eirene.html.

2. John F. Hart, "John," in *The Moody Bible Commentary,* ed. Michael A. Rydelnik and Michael Vanlaningham (Chicago, IL: Moody Publishers, 2014), 1605–1606.

Session Two

1. *The Expositor's Bible Commentary,* vol. 9, ed. Frank E. Gaebelein (Grand Rapids, MI: The Zondervan Corporation, 1981), 29.

2. Rosaria Butterfield, *The Gospel Comes with a House Key: Practicing Radically Ordinary Hospitality in Our Post-Christian World* (Crossway, 2018). Accessed on Audible.

3. *The Expositor's Bible Commentary,* 29.

4. Ibid., 40.

5. Ibid.

6. Ibid., 41.

7. R. C. Sproul, *John: An Expositional Commentary* (Sanford, FL: Ligonier Ministries, 2009), 20.

8. *Zondervan Illustrated Bible Backgrounds Commentary,* vol. 2A, eds., Craig S. Keener (Grand Rapids, MI: Zondervan, 2019), 21.

9. R. C. Sproul, "The Wedding at Cana," Ligonier Ministries, Jan. 19, 2018. Available at www.ligonier.org/learn/devotionals/wedding-at-cana.

10. Keener, 21. Also see Edward W. Klink III, *John: Exegetical Commentary on the New Testament* (Grand Rapids, MI: Zondervan Academic, 2016), 164.

11. Ibid.

12. Sproul, 22.

13. Keener, 23.

14. Warren W. Wiersbe, *Be Alive* (Colorado Springs, CO: David C Cook, 2009), 43.

15. *"Pisteuo,"* Bible Study Tools, accessed Oct. 16, 2023. Available at www.biblestudytools.com/lexicons/greek/nas/pisteuo.html.

16. Ibid.

17. Wiersbe, 52.

18. Sproul, 37.

19. Keener, 30.

20. Sproul, 44.

21. Ibid., 56.

22. D. A. Carson, *The Gospel According to John* (Grand Rapids, MI: Wm. B. Eerdmans Publishing Company, 1991), 211.

Session Three

1. Kenneth E. Bailey, *Jesus Through Middle Eastern Eyes* (Downers Grove, IL: InterVarsity Press, 2008), 201.

2. Ibid., 202.

3. Ibid., 203.

4. Ibid., 202.

5. Klink, 261.

6. Ibid., 271.

7. Weirsbe, 79.

8. Gerald L. Borchert, *The New American Commentary, John 1–11,* vol. 25A (Nashville, TN: Broadman & Holman Publishers, 1996). Accessed through Logos Bible Software. Available at www.logos.com.

9. "Eschatology," *Merriam-Webster's Dictionary,* accessed Oct. 16, 2023. Available at www.merriam-webster.com/dictionary/eschatology.

10. Wiersbe, 85.

11. Ibid., 86.

12. Warren W. Wiersbe, *Warren Wiersbe BE Bible Study Series,* Bible Gateway, accessed Oct. 17, 2023. Available at www.biblegateway.com/resources/wiersbe-be-bible-study/3-he-claimed-that-there-are-valid-witnesses-who.

13. Klink, 303.

14. Ibid., 304.

15. Ibid., 311.

16. Leon Morris, *The Gospel According to John* (Grand Rapids, MI: Wm. B. Eerdmans Publishing Co., 1989), 361.

17. "*Mathetes*," Bible Study Tools, accessed Oct. 19, 2023. Available at www.biblestudytools.com/lexicons/greek/nas/mathetes.html.

Session Four

1. Keener, 66.

2. "*Skenoo*," Bible Study Tools, accessed Sept. 5, 2023. Available at www.biblestudytools.com/lexicons/greek/nas/skenoo.html.

3. Klink, 357.

4. Eli Lizorkin-Eyzenberg, *The Jewish Gospel of John: Discovering Jesus, King of All Israel* (Lizorkin-Eyzenberg, 2015–2019), 119.

5. Matt Carter and Josh Wredberg, *Christ-Centered Exposition Commentary: Exalting Jesus in John* (Nashville, TN: B&H Publishing Group, 2017), 179.

6. Keener, 75.

7. Bailey, 229.

8. Ibid., 57, 233–235.

9. Sproul, 141.

10. Ibid.

11. Ibid.

12. "Surprising facts about phobias," Aruma, accessed Oct. 20, 2023. Available at www.aruma.com.au/about-us/blog/surprising-facts-about-phobias.

13. Carson, 337.

14. Wiersbe, 126.

15. Gaebelein, 92.

16. Carson, 345.

17. Klink, 441.

18. Ibid., 439.

19. Ibid., 430.

20. Keener, 93.

21. Klink, 444.

22. Keener, 97.

Session Five

1. Keener, 101.

2. Morris, 501.

3. Ibid., 502.

4. Carson, 382.

5. Morris, 503.

6. "*Perissos*," Bible Study Tools, accessed Oct. 20, 2023. Available at www.biblestudytools.com/lexicons/greek/nas/perissos.html.

7. Carson, 381.

8. Morris, 509.

9. Carson, 391.

10. Gaebelein, 118.

11. Ibid., 119.

12. Ibid.

13. Carter, 234.

14. Carson, 430.

15. Ibid., 429.

16. Ibid., 433.

17. Ibid., 437.

18. Klink, 571.

19. Alyssa Roat, "What Does Agape Love Really Mean in the Bible?" Christianity.com, accessed Oct. 20, 2023. Available at www.christianity.com/wiki/christian-terms/what-does-agape-love-really-mean-in-the-bible.html.

20. Morris, 625; Keener, 141.

21. Keener, 142.

22. John MacArthur, *The MacArthur New Testament, John 12–21* (Chicago: Moody Publishers, 2008). Accessed through Logos Bible Software. Available at www.logos.com.

23. Carson, 473.

Session Six

1. Gaebelein, 143.

2. Klink, 615.

3. Lizorkin, 193.

4. Chip Ingram, "How to Pray When Anxiety Knocks at Your Heart," Living on the Edge, accessed Oct. 21, 2023. Available at https://livingontheedge.org/2018/04/30/how-to-pray-when-anxiety-knocks-at-your-heart.

5. Sproul, 252.

6. Gaebelein, 146.

7. Warren W. Wiersbe, *Be Transformed, John 13–21* (Colorado Springs, CO: David C Cook, 1986), 41.

8. Carson, 498.

9. Ibid., "*Eirene*," Bible Study Tools.

10. "*Shalowm*," Biblestudytools.com, accessed Sept. 8, 2023. Available at www.biblestudytools.com.

11. Carson, 506.

12. Ralph Gower, *The New Manners and Customs of Bible Times* (Chicago: Moody Press, 1987), 106.

13. "*Meno*," Biblestudytools.com, accessed Sept. 9, 2023. Available online at www.biblestudytools.com/lexicons/greek/nas/meno.html.

14. *The MacArthur New Testament, John 12–21.*

15. Morris, 716.

16. Gaebelein, 164.

Session Seven

1. "*Passion* (n.)," Online Etymology Dictionary, accessed Oct. 20, 2023. Available online at www.etymonline.com/word/passion.

2. Wiersbe, 106.

3. Ibid., 111.

4. "Matthew 27:16," *Gill's Exposition of the Entire Bible,* Bible Hub, accessed Oct. 23, 2023. Available at https://biblehub.com/commentaries/matthew/27-16.htm.

5. Keener, 184.

6. Carson, 597; Morris, 790.

7. Carson, 608.

8. Ibid., 610.

9. Carson, 615; Gaebelein, 182.

10. Morris, 807.

11. Wiersbe, 140.

12. Morris, 814.

13. Keener, 197.

14. Sproul, 352.

15. J. Ramsey Michaels, *The New International Commentary on the New Testament, The Gospel of John* (Grand Rapids, MI: William B. Eerdmans Publishing Company, 2010). Accessed through Logos Bible Software. Available at www.logos.com.

16. Keener, 204.

17. Gerald L. Borchert, *The New American Commentary, John 12–21,* vol. 25 (Nashville, TN: Broadman & Holman Publishers, 2002). Accessed through Logos Bible Software. Available at www.logos.com.

18. Kenneth O. Gangel, *Holman New Testament Commentary,* Max Anders, ed. (Nashville, TN: Broadman & Holman Publishers, 2000). Accessed through Logos Bible Software. Available at www.logos.com.

19. Keener, 208.

20. Gaebelein, 201.

21. Morris, 873.

22. Carson, 678; Wiersbe, 182; Keener, 211; Morris, 873.

23. Carson, 680; Wiersbe, 184; Keener, 212.

24. Wiersbe, 181.

VIDEO VIEWER GUIDE ANSWERS

Session One

create
90
old age
Jewish
Person
fascination
pray

Session Two

unfailing
Savior
story
actionable
subjects
glory

Session Three

significant
fix / heart
Asking / believing
Spiritual / physical
appetites / nourishment
Bread

Session Four

source / satisfaction
surface / correctly
spiritual thirst
thirsty
living water / cisterns
shame
spiritual sight

Session Five

purposes / circumstances
bummer / abundant
shepherd / need
outcomes / listening
control
good / Good Shepherd's
glorify
believe

Session Six

fallible / inevitable
defend
intercede / issues
intercede
Advocate
sustain
for / with

Session Seven

toward / away
dishonor / honor
believe
work
stays

NOTES

NOTES

NOTES

NOTES

LET'S BE FRIENDS!

BLOG

We're here to help you grow in your faith, develop as a leader, and find encouragement as you go.

lifewaywomen.com

SOCIAL

Find inspiration in the in-between moments of life.

@lifewaywomen

NEWSLETTER

Be the first to hear about new studies, events, giveaways, and more by signing up.

lifeway.com/womensnews

APP

Download the Lifeway Women app for Bible study plans, online study groups, a prayer wall, and more!

 Google Play   App Store

Lifeway women

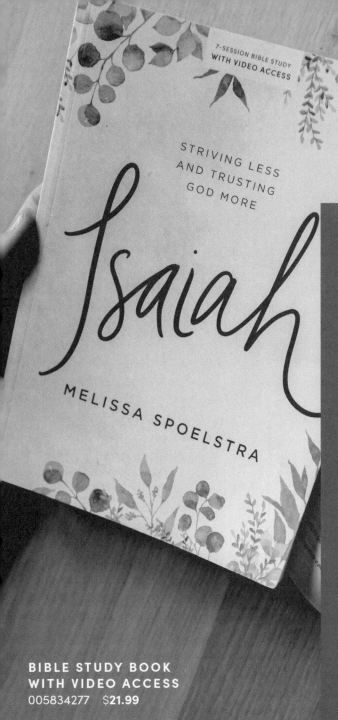

7-SESSION BIBLE STUDY
WITH VIDEO ACCESS

STRIVING LESS
AND TRUSTING
GOD MORE

Isaiah

MELISSA SPOELSTRA

**BIBLE STUDY BOOK
WITH VIDEO ACCESS**
005834277   **$21.99**

lifeway.com/isaiah | 800.458.2772

Lifeway. women

Psalms 66-68

THOSE WHO TRUST IN THE *LORD* WILL FIND NEW STRENGTH.

Isaiah 40:31a, NLT

Isaiah's message echoes into our lives today as we read his call to rely on the Lord. Using the genres of poetry, narrative, and prophecy, Isaiah communicated clearly that followers of God can trust in Him.

In this 7-session study of the book of Isaiah, learn to rest in God's promises and grow in trust. Unpacking Isaiah's words—from the prophet's challenging words to the nation of Israel to his prophecies of the Messiah to come — will reveal that you can trust God more than your own human effort or the counterfeits the world suggests. You won't be striving harder, but instead trusting more deeply the Faithful One who is so worthy of your utter dependence. In Him you'll find the comfort and peace you need to sustain you.

Get the most from your study.

In this study you'll:

- Understand that peace is not a program or perspective; peace is a person

- Embrace the gift of peace Jesus promises

- Slow down your busy life and learn to walk in the pace of Jesus

- Discover the distinctions of John's Gospel through context and historical insights

To enrich your study experience, consider the accompanying video teaching sessions from Melissa Spoelstra, approximately 25–30 minutes each.

STUDYING ON YOUR OWN?

Watch Melissa Spoelstra's teaching sessions, available via redemption code for individual video-streaming access, printed in this Bible study book.

LEADING A GROUP?

Each group member will need *The Gospel of John* Bible Study Book, which includes video access. Because all participants will have access to the video content, you can choose to watch the videos outside of your group meeting if desired. Or, if you're watching together and someone misses a group meeting, they'll have the flexibility to catch up! A DVD set is also available to purchase separately if desired.

Browse study formats, a free session sample, video clips, church promotional materials, and more at

lifeway.com/gospelofjohn